COMMON-SENSE
BUSINESS STRATEGY

COMMON-SENSE BUSINESS STRATEGY

How to improve your profits
and cash flow dramatically

Barrie Pearson
Livingstone Fisher Plc

MERCURY

First published in hardback in 1987 by Mercury Books
Reprinted   January 1988
              October 1988
              November 1990

Reprinted in paperback November 1991
by Mercury Books, Gold Arrow Publications Ltd,
862 Garratt Lane, London SW17 0NB

Set in Plantin and Univers by Phoenix Photosetting
Printed and bound in Great Britain by
Mackays of Chatham PLC, Chatham, Kent

Cartoons by Ken Pyne

British Library Cataloguing in Publication Data

Pearson, Barrie
    Common-sense business strategy: how to improve
    your profits and cash flow dramatically
    1. Success in business
    I. Title
    650.1   HF5386

ISBN 1-85252-099-X

To Catherine . . . .

For her common sense, and especially her love.

PREFACE

Corporate planning is dead and nearly buried. Long live commercial common sense!

Millions of managers and business owners have read books and attended seminars on strategy, but few people do manage their businesses strategically, and they tend to have become millionaires! These people use strategic common sense, not complex planning techniques. Common-sense strategy shows you how to create your own success story by achieving a quantum jump improvement in results.

Planning techniques have become so complicated that they are the preserve of 'planning experts'. The result in many companies has been long-winded business plans filed and forgotten almost as soon as they have been written, which is nonsense.

This book is based on over 10 years of experience gained from advising and working with chief executives, entrepreneurs and partners in professional firms. Their aim was to produce a quantum jump in the results achieved by their business. They wanted a better way to manage, not more sophisticated planning techniques to be used once or twice a year, and they achieved their goal by developing a common-sense approach for managing their business strategically.

The aim of this book is to share these strategic-management techniques with readers. The book gives a practical and down-to-earth 'how to' guide to help people define winning strategies for their business, then it shows 'how to' implement those strategies successfully. Translating strategy into tangible results is a crucial step, often one where businesses come unstuck.

These techniques are widely applicable. They have been adapted successfully in businesses ranging from household name multi-nationals to a professional firm with only two partners.

This book has been written for every manager wanting to achieve outstanding results. These include chief executives of large groups and subsidiary companies, entrepreneurs, owners, partners in professional firms, directors, business-development executives – in fact managers everywhere.

The contents include taking stock of the present situation, adopting a quantum jump approach, developing a vision for success, assessing external trends, identifying crucial issues to be tackled, overcoming obstacles, the importance of people, using a workshop approach to strategic management, setting key business-development projects, measuring milestones of achievement, and selling the strategy to people. Numerous real-life situations are described to show how the approach works, though some of them have had to be disguised.

Nicole Musikant, my secretary, did a splendid job to turn a hand-written draft into the finished book.

This is a book to be read and acted on, and used again and again.

Livingstone Fisher Plc,   BARRIE PEARSON
Acre House, 11–15 William Road,
London NW1 3ER

CONTENTS

CONTENTS

CONTENTS

1 HOW TO MANAGE STRATEGICALLY, USING COMMON SENSE

It seems that business has never been tougher than today, and is likely to get more so. Owners and managers already work long and hard, but working longer and harder is no guarantee for success, not even survival. More effective management is needed, and this requires a strategic approach.

People confuse work with results. Work in fact is often allowed to become an obstacle to achieving outstanding results. Many executives spend most of their time doing work which could be done at least as well and more cheaply by one of their staff. Not surprisingly these are the people who complain that they do not have time to invest in the future success of the business.

Chief executives, business owners and partners in professional firms must make time to create a vision of success for their business. They need to define the future direction of the business in terms of commercial rationale and priorities. The issues which are crucial to the success of the business must be identified and tackled vigorously. Work must not be allowed to get in the way of future success.

If only business was allowed to be this simple! The subsidiaries and divisions of large companies often suffer bureaucratic and time-wasting corporate-planning procedures imposed by head office. Business owners and partners in professional firms allow themselves to be swamped by daily work.

After lecturing to thousands of directors and working with dozens of corporate clients as a management consultant, I have found that

1

one thing has become clear: whilst strategic management techniques are widely known, many people have a marked lack of ability to manage strategically. Yet they come to seminars looking for the latest techniques as if to find a panacea.

Strategic management is simple, old-fashioned and must not be allowed to become complicated. Successful businessmen are street-wise and commercial; they are unlikely to spend time using sophisticated planning techniques.

Comments made by the chief executives or directors of three companies with household names, each with annual sales of more than £1 billion, illustrate the problem:

> When I joined the company, I inherited a corporate planning process which was nothing more than the most expensive and inaccurate forecasting system in Christendom (chief executive, food and beverage company).

> Our annual business planning is used by several subsidiaries to attempt to justify financing them to continue doing more of the same, when major new initiatives are needed (chief executive of a group which has divested itself of several subsidiaries since then).

> I've just suffered the annual pain of submitting the business plan for the next five years for my subsidiaries. At least it gets head office off my back (main board director, engineering group).

A fundamental misunderstanding

There is a widespread belief that operational management, the day-to-day hard work, is separate and different from strategic management, which is often seen as thinking about long-term issues. This is a fundamental misunderstanding of the essence of management.

Management covers the whole spectrum from the immediate to

long-term issues. It is not the timescale or horizon which makes something a strategic matter, but its importance to corporate success or even survival. Strategic issues may require desperately urgent action.

The case of a substantial professional firm in London illustrates the point. The business was continuing to expand because the amount of incoming work was ample. Its technical reputation was sound, its commitment to client service was good, and its fee rates were competitive. It was seen as a successful firm by clients and other professional firms. The reality was totally different.

There was a cash-flow crisis facing the firm. The overdraft was the maximum the bank would tolerate. The bank was demanding personal guarantees from the partners, using their homes as security. Creditors, including income tax and value added taxes, were long overdue for payment, and legal action was imminent.

Significant amounts of work were done for clients on a speculative basis, and only a minority of these became fee-paying assignments. Jobs were often won by quoting the lowest price; the control of work was poor, often resulting in unprofitable jobs, and little attempt was made to agree interim invoicing with clients. Final invoices were not sent out promptly when assignments were completed.

The initial rescue action was immediate and mundane, but of strategic importance. For a short while each partner spent his mornings:

- personally telephoning each of his clients whose payment was overdue (previously cash collection had been handled by account clerks, who occasionally sent out statements if other work allowed time to do this)

- resolving any reasons or excuses for non-payment; and visiting the client if necessary

- invoicing all jobs which had been completed and not invoiced

- agreeing interim invoicing with the client on current jobs where possible, and despatching the invoices promptly

This action ensured the survival of the firm and was the catalyst that converted the business to strategic managment.

COMMON-SENSE BUSINESS STRATEGY

Why bother with strategic management?

Most of the businesses wanting help with strategic management are in difficulty or can see problems looming. Successful companies, small businesses and professional firms may not see the need or the benefits of adopting strategic management, but the reasons for doing so are powerful. Past and present success provide no guarantee of future prospects, particularly in the rapidly changing and uncertain business world of today. Changes in technology, legislation, energy prices, competition and suchlike may require different strategies to ensure continued success.

Professional firms are facing dramatic changes, and strategic management is essential. An evolutionary approach is not enough to ensure survival. Advertising rules are being relaxed, competition is coming from different quarters, and major firms are diversifying to offer their clients a comprehensive range of services. Medium-sized firms are being squeezed as larger competitors pursue smaller clients. Small firms have to seek new clients to maintain a reasonable income for their partners.

Working harder may make people luckier. Strategic management makes them more successful, and may require less work.

The quantum jump approach

A quantum jump means a big improvement. Many owners and managers plan to achieve only a small improvement in results each year, even if present performance is barely adequate. For example, a regional newspaper company took it for granted that as their local newspaper circulation generally had declined steadily for years, this would continue. So they planned simply to minimise the decline in circulation. Strategic management rejects this negative approach completely and sets goals which demand a substantial achievement.

Some people set goals requiring a quantum jump in results, even arbitrarily, and then create a vision to achieve them. Others will define their vision and then set the results to be achieved. Both methods work, provided that the vision and the results to be achieved are compatible.

A strategic approach takes a circular path, which can be started at different points, as shown in Figure 1 overleaf. Such an approach is essential to achieve a quantum jump in results, but not enough.

A quantum jump means a big improvement

Strategic action must follow, because evolution is likely to be inadequate, so a few major business-development projects need to be carried out to turn the vision into tangible achievement. These projects will focus on those issues which are crucial to business success, e.g. marketing, selling, manufacturing, research, distribution, finance, organisation structure, recruitment or whatever else is relevant.

FIGURE 1. CIRCULARITY OF STRATEGIC APPROACH

Explore opportunities

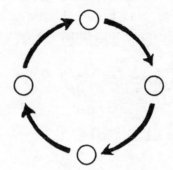

Set results
to achieve

Identify and
evaluate options

Create vision
for success

Action summary

1. Make time to create a vision for success, and don't confuse work with results.

2. Demand a quantum jump in results.

3. Identify the crucial issues and opportunities for success, and concentrate on them.

4. Set major business-development projects to turn the vision into tangible achievement. Don't rely on evolution for success.

2 HOW TO LAY THE FOUNDATIONS FOR SUCCESS

An outstandingly successful business needs a sound foundation, which ensures that simple but vitally important day-to-day matters are consistently handled well. This chapter gives a brief reminder of some of the things which require constant attention but are often allowed to slip.

Sales opportunities

People have a tendency to think that diversification is more attractive, and miss sales opportunities within their existing business and customer base as a result. For instance, when the customer is a subsidiary of a group of companies, the opportunity should be taken to ask for either an introduction to someone, or at least the name of a person to contact, either at group level or in other subsidiary companies, in search of business.

Many companies list their most important customers in the order of invoiced sales, and understandably so, but it may be more important to list major customers and non-customers in the order of *potential* sales value, and alongside each one to record actual sales. Large differences between potential and actual sales to a customer should be analysed in order to understand the reasons, and a sales attack mounted. Quite often a customer buys only some of the product range. An analysis of sales by product type to major customers will highlight these situations, so that efforts can be made to sell the remainder of the range equally effectively.

Cross-selling is not done as systematically as it deserves. Subsidiary companies in a group should be cross-selling by exchanging client lists and providing personal introductions wherever appropriate for other subsidiaries.

Former customers and clients often do not get the attention they deserve. It is important to know promptly that someone has become a former customer, so that action may be taken before the competition entrenches itself. Some professional firms perform one-off services for their clients, such as a house purchase or a patent application, but do not keep in contact in order to build a continuing business relationship.

Consider potential sales value of non-customers

New product ideas may sometimes arise from the needs of seemingly demanding or difficult customers, in service industries as well as in highly technical fields such as electronics or biotechnology. A corporate client of my company commissioned the design of a seminar to train major systems salesmen in the use of discounted cash-flow awareness to help to sell the financial benefits, because no suitable training programme was available. He then invited us to sell it as a public seminar if we wished.

Customer service

We live in what seems to be increasingly a *self-service* world. When a service is provided, therefore, it is more noticeable and appreciated today.

Often good service is inexpensive or even cost-free to provide. It does require, however, a company-wide belief and commitment to provide outstanding service. Not just the salesmen, but everyone dealing with a customer must regard themselves as an ambassador for the company. Telephonists, secretaries, receptionists, and delivery drivers are an integral part of the customer service.

Staff attitudes are crucial. Company-wide training programmes may be needed to bring about the required awareness and commitment to service. Airlines and railway companies, for example, have put tens of thousands of their employees through specially tailored programmes. It is desirable to reinforce this kind of training with specific campaigns to improve customer service. People must feel it is part of their job to provide good service, and be continually reminded of its importance.

Measurable standards are needed for customer service, and performance should be measured regularly. Standards should be set for those few key features which are important to the customer; too many different standards of service to aim for are likely to diminish the response from employees.

Service standards for a railway might simply be the following:

- over 95 per cent of all trains will arrive at their destination within 5 minutes of schedule

- each carriage will be cleaned before the journey begins

- restaurant and buffet services will be provided as advertised on over 95 per cent of trains

- queuing time for tickets will not exceed 3 minutes, or 6 minutes during designated peak hours

If there is doubt about what customers regard as important, then surveys or questionnaires should be used to determine their requirements.

By measuring the service provided, important selling features may be obtained. A motoring organisation has used the fact that eight out of ten breakdown calls are attended to within an hour of notification as part of an advertising campaign to attract new members. Speed of service response is equally important to a wide range of customers from television set owners to corporate computer users.

Some customer complaints are inevitable. There is no doubt, however, that speedy and effective handling of a complaint may result in a satisfied and loyal customer. Once again, standards must be set and measured regularly. Equally money must be invested in training staff to ensure that complaints are handled well.

Quality and reliability are strong selling features. The whole workforce needs to be aware of how important these are. Continuous training and the wish to give good service are needed to maintain quality standards.

Service operations require particular attention. It is not enough to have the required standard at the beginning of the day, and then to allow things to deteriorate. Standards need to be set and monitored regularly. Attention to detail is important. For example, one chain of motorway cafés checks the lavatories every hour for cleanliness, and each check is recorded to ensure the discipline is maintained.

Quality circles have been publicised widely and used successfully in many manufacturing operations. The concept is just as applicable to service companies, but does not seem to have been used to the same extent.

Business image

Every business has an image, even if no one makes a conscious attempt to create or improve it. The image is created not just by the product and service, but by everything that the customer sees and experiences.

First impressions do count

First impressions do count. So things such as the reception area, letters and promotional literature are important.

Sometimes the reception area is unwelcoming, untidy, shabby, even used for temporary storage of office supplies. It should contain product samples or display boards, company and product literature, the annual reports of the company, award certificates won and anything else that helps to create the desired image. Some of the worst reception areas and letterheadings are to be found amongst the smallest professional firms. As their 'product' is meeting people to give advice which is confirmed in writing, there is no excuse.

Letterheadings need to be designed and not left to the printer offering the cheapest price. Equally the quality of paper used and the standard of typing or word-processing need to be good. Large companies invest in design, but small companies wrongly tend to look upon design as an avoidable expense rather than a source of extra sales and profitability.

Design in the widest sense is not just part of an intangible company image, but can lead to dramatic increases in sales and profits. Customers do look for better designed products and often are prepared to pay a premium price for them. The presentation of products can have a tremendous impact on sales, and there are numerous examples of dramatic increases in sales of existing products as a result of repackaging. Equally shop and store design as a total concept can produce similar results.

Cost reduction

Turning off the lights whenever one leaves the office is common sense, but cost reduction needs to be tackled with *strategic* common sense to be effective. A desirable aim must be to become the lowest cost producer for a given specification of goods or services. This allows either more to be spent on marketing and selling or higher profit margins at any given market price for the item to be achieved.

Value analysis should be used to challenge the specification of products. The customer buys the product or service for the benefit of using it or the pleasure of owning it, and if the specification is unnecessarily high for the purpose intended, then the product cost is higher than it needs to be.

Value analysis should also be used to attack the cost of significant items of expenditure, and not just in production departments. For example, management information is deceptively costly to produce, and should be subjected to value analysis.

Employment costs and items of expenditure not directly concerned with making, distributing or selling the products and services should be subjected to particular scrutiny. The existence of service departments should be challenged and alternatives examined. Should staff catering be handed over to a specialist catering company? Is it cost-effective for the company to repair its own lorries and cars? Could more expert tax advice be obtained, at a similar cost, by using specialist external tax advisers rather than having an internal department? Why are internal painters and decorators employed? Should product delivery be completely, or partly, subcontracted?

Similar questions could be asked of numerous other peripheral activities. Not only cost, but the drain on management time should be considered when deciding whether or not to make a change.

Offices in the centre of major cities, whether owned or leased, are expensive. Whilst a prestigious or convenient city-centre presence may be needed or desirable, the number of people located there should be kept to an absolute minimum. For example, the group financial accounting staff do *not* need to be located in a city centre to produce consolidated accounts.

Asset and cash management

Managers should manage assets and not imagine that these should be left to the accountants to handle. The reality is, however, that too ny managers concern themselves only with profit. Assets which managers should manage include debtors, inventory, fixed and surplus assets, and equity investments.

Debtors

Amongst professonal partnerships and small businesses debtor-management is often poor. The starting point for cash collection is to prepare and despatch invoices promptly, and interim invoicing should be agreed with the customer or client whenever appropriate. In some circumstances a deposit should be requested at the outset, and this is appropriate for the provision of professional services as well as for the supply of products. Outstanding debts need to be chased as soon as they become due for payment. The reason for non-payment needs establishing quickly and dealing with promptly, because standard follow-up letters are often ignored. For example, a query concerning the amount to be paid may be used as an excuse for not paying. The first telephone call to chase an overdue payment should establish the reason or excuse for delay. Partners and directors should know each month the number of debtor days outstanding; an increase of only 1 or 2 days needs prompt action to retrieve the situation.

Inventory

The inventory levels for raw materials, work-in-progress and finished goods stocks are the responsibility of line managers. Standards need to be set and monitored.

Stock levels should be set in relation to anticipated sales, which may be quite different from recent experience. Unsaleable stock should be disposed of and space released. In many inventories 10 per cent of the number of lines account for up to 90 per cent of total stock by value. Clearly the key items of stock by value need to be identified and managed tightly.

Fixed assets

Within the medium term the cash invested in some fixed assets may be 'unfixed'. Existing property could be sold and leased back. A fleet of vehicles could be sold to a leasing company and leased back. Equally future acquisitions of property, equipment and vehicles could be leased. Strategic common sense means that the options should be examined and appropriate action taken as part of a sensible approach to financing the business.

Surplus assets

Surplus buildings, or even vacant floorspace within a building, are apparent to everyone and action is usually taken. Surplus equipment and stocks are often allowed to remain for years, using up valuable floorspace.

If the stock really is unsaleable or unusable in the normal course of trade, then it should be disposed of at the best price obtainable. A newly appointed divisional manager of an oil company, finding he had inherited a huge stock of redundant replacement parts for the processing plant, sold it for over £7 million in cash. The accountants had written off nearly all the value in an earlier year, so the manager boosted his profit as well as his cash flow.

A paper manufacturer decided to close an old plant, even though it was in good working order, because quality standards had improved in recent years beyond the capability of the equipment. The initial assumption was that the cost of removing it from the site would be greater than the scrap value, but the chief executive intervened and instructed people to find a buyer. Enquiry quickly revealed a secondhand equipment broker who had a ready buyer in a developing country.

Equity investments

Companies take minority equity stakes in both quoted and unquoted companies from time to time, no doubt for sound commercial reasons at the outset. Over the years the reasons for and benefits from the investment may disappear because the circumstances change. Whilst a moderate dividend yield may have been acceptable when other benefits were being obtained, today it may make sense to realise the investment and use the cash to develop wholly owned businesses. Nonetheless some companies never seem to review their minority equity investments.

Action summary

1. Identify and action sales opportunities with major customers by comparing actual and potential sales to each one.

2. Ask subsidiary company customers to provide an introduction to pursue sales opportunities throughout their group.

3. Ask other subsidiaries in your group to introduce you to their customers.

4. Plan to become the lowest cost producer for a given specification of product or service.

5. Set measurable standards for customer service and product quality, and monitor performance regularly.

6. Plan to improve your corporate image and presentation to customers.

7. Remember that line managers should manage fixed assets and working capital.

8. Identify and sell off redundant fixed assets and stock, which are often allowed to remain for years before action is taken.

9. Review the reasons for and benefits from retaining minority equity stakes in other companies, and consider realising the investments and using the cash to develop wholly owned businesses.

3 HOW TO TAKE STOCK OF YOUR MARKET PLACE

'Gut feel' can be valuable in identifying market opportunities, but sound strategies are based on as much tangible evidence as can reasonably be obtained. We all like to think that we know our market well, but our views are often based on impressions. When a company systematically gathers hard facts about the market place for the first time, the analysis is likely to provide some surprises.

Taking stock of your market place requires the following steps:

- identifying market segments and geographical territories

    – you serve at present
    – you should consider entering

- Evaluating each one by

    – analysing the relevant history
    – identifying and evaluating trends and likely developments
    – compiling future projections

Identifying market segments and geographical territories

A market segment is a part of a market which can be segregated or differentiated from the rest of the market, e.g. in terms of customer type, product usage or distribution channel. The size of the market

Market segments need to be defined

segment or geographical territory needs to be measurable for it to be meaningful.

Perceptive identification of market segments may be highly revealing in terms of the effectiveness of penetration. For example, the market for computerised building-management systems can be segmented into new buildings and existing ones, and each of these can be further segmented into, say, public buildings, retail outlets, industrial premises and offices. Even further segmentation may be useful. It may reveal that, say, school premises are the largest and fastest growing segment within the existing public buildings sector. Segments of a market are likely to differ widely from each other in terms of growth and competition, and the share of different segments in a market a company has is likely to vary equally widely. The analysis should be used to focus the marketing and sales efforts of the company on the most attractive segments.

Attractive new market segments emerge and a competitive advantage may be gained by identifying them and responding quickly. For example, the advent of home computers created a new market segment for specialist magazines catering for enthusiasts.

Some large consumer-product companies regard the whole world as one geographic territory. They have created powerful, worldwide brands, using similar marketing, advertising and selling approaches in different countries. This has become necessary to combat the increasing concentration of merchant power resulting from take-overs in the retail trade in various countries. Consequently retail chains' own-label brands have become large enough to be supported by extensive press and television advertising. As own-labels tend to be nationwide or restricted to within a continent, rather than global, the worldwide brands have the inherent advantages of the economies of the larger scale. In the United Kingdom worldwide brands such as Heinz and Nescafé compete with the own-label brand of Sainsbury's supermarkets, and Sony and Panasonic compete with the own-label products of the Dixons retail chain.

Geography is changing in terms of commercial opportunities. Countries such as South Korea and the Republic of China have encouraged wide-ranging trade initiatives in recent years. For example, in the mid-eighties China invited two major insurance brokers to visit the country as a first step to developing trading links with them, but a few years earlier such a move would have seemed highly improbable. Hong Kong is a territory where foreign service companies and professional firms have recognised the business opportunities for people prepared to establish an office there.

Within individual countries opportunities have arisen from the local concentration of new industries. Silicon Valley in California is well known. More recently, Cambridge in England has attracted technological companies by creating a science park, a site with buildings and facilities designed to attract high-technology companies to relocate there. Service businesses such as accountants and patents agents have been keen to establish regional offices in the Cambridge area to seize the local opportunity.

The key is to recognise which geographical territories are likely to offer attractive opportunities and to be one of the first companies to pursue them.

Analysing relevant history

The aim should be to understand quantitatively what has happened, and the reasons why.

Sales revenue figures are likely to be available for each market sector covering recent years. Further analysis into units sold and selling prices should be possible. Within particular market segments, however, data may be harder to obtain. Indirect indicators should be used where necessary to make informed estimates for market segments rather than leave gaps in the analysis.

Underlying factors should be identified and evaluated to discover the key determinants of market changes in volume, unit price and total revenue terms. The underlying factors may be social changes, which are often imperceptible when considered daily, weekly or monthly, but add up to a significant change over several years. Some of the important social changes are concerned with the changing family unit, working women, and lack of population growth.

The changing family unit

The percentage of married couples making up households declined significantly in the UK and the USA during the seventies. Less than two-thirds of households in each country are now married couples, producing growing market segments for other types of household. The change has resulted from a marked trend towards more divorces and fewer marriages, which has contributed to the need for more women to work and to become financially independent.

Working women

Since 1970 the percentage of working women in the total workforce has increased significantly in the USA and European countries. This has contributed to significant changes in eating habits. Sales of fast foods, take-away and convenience foods have grown sharply. McDonalds, Pizza Hut and others have spread internationally. Ready prepared chilled meals, increasingly branded and using fresh ingredients rather than frozen ones, have grown in popularity.

Lack of population growth

The trend in the USA and European countries has been towards population growth of only 1 per cent a year or even less. This does not mean that the market is static. As people live longer, there are significant shifts between the various age groups: retired people are an increasing proportion of the population, whilst children are a decreasing one. The different rates of growth or decline are further accentuated by differing levels of disposable income amongst the various age groups.

In some countries demographic change is well documented in national census surveys. Regional population shifts may highlight changes in local market opportunities. In addition ownership of telephones, cars, freezers, video-recorders and suchlike may be reported, together with the consumption of tea, beer, wine, biscuits, cigarettes, and so on. This factual data and the trends revealed are too valuable to ignore.

Other factors which may have influenced changes in the market place include changes in:

- currency conversion rates

- inflation

- bank interest rates

- oil prices

- legislation, e.g. compulsory vehicle seat belts
- dumping from overseas suppliers

Trends and likely developments

Recent history may be an unreliable indicator of future trends. The steady rise in oil prices, followed by a sharp decrease during 1986, is one example. The aim should be to identify those trends and anticipated developments which are likely to offer the chance to swim with the tide of opportunity, rather than against it.

. . . Swim with the tide of opportunity

The issues which need to be considered include:

- social change
- economic trends
- technological development
- political factors
- anticipated legislation
- consumerism and pressure groups

These will be considered in turn.

Social change

Some examples of social change have already been addressed earlier in this chapter as part of the analysis of relevant history.

Many trends arising from social change are long-lived, and the key assumption to be made is the rate of change to be expected in the future. Rising crime rates in many countries provide an example, creating opportunities for the security industry. In terms of market opportunities, however, a commercial lead can be gained by identifying emerging social trends and responding to them before the competiton does. For example, the worldwide popularisation of marathon running in recent years has been part of the pursuit of physical exercise. It has created a demand for specialist sportswear and magazines, and offered sponsorship opportunities with wide media coverage.

Economic trends

The aim is to identify the market segments and geographic territories which are likely to offer above-average prospects of profitable growth, so that the business can be repostured towards the more attractive segments and territories, and become less dependent on the declining ones. Factors to be considered will include gross national income, levels of disposable income, currency levels, anticipated inflation rates, commodity and raw material availability, and energy costs.

Technological development

Technological developments from outside an industry often have substantially more impact than those arising within the industry sector. For instance, the impact of the silicon chip on watch manufacture, the real prices of watches, and distribution channels used to sell them has been dramatic since the earlier 1970s. Accurate and reliable watches are now sold in petrol stations as an impulse buy. The effect on prices and distribution channels has been as fundamental as on manufacturing methods.

Technological developments which are likely to have a wide-ranging impact include:

- biotechnology
- genetic engineering
- laser beams
- very large scale integrated circuits
- artificial intelligence
- optical fibres
- space satellites

Companies need to be technologically aware. Even the smallest businesses should scan the technology pages of the relevant national and trade press, and larger companies will want to take up some of the new technologies. Some of the major food companies have entered biotechnology because of the substantial impact likely on the source of ingredients and the preservation of food. Links and joint ventures with university research departments may be well worthwhile.

Political factors

People tend to think that political influences are likely to pose threats rather than to create opportunities. Equally, small companies are likely to feel that only big business is able to consider the impact of political factors. Neither view is correct.

The key is awareness. For the small business this may mean no more than reading a quality newspaper and the trade press to spot what is happening, or, better still, what is being proposed. Where a country is an important export market for a small company, then obtaining free reports on request from the bank, or simply being aware of the need to keep informed when talking to overseas agents and customers is probably sufficient.

Political influences provide opportunities as well as threats to companies whether large or small. For example, government finance for inner-city restoration may provide local opportunities for a small company providing specialist cleaning services for buildings to remove the years of grime which have discoloured the external stonework.

Political influences which may affect a company include:

- local initiatives by city councils or governing bodies
- inner-city or regional aid
- anticipated change of government locally or nationally
- tariff changes and trade embargoes
- nationalisation or privatisation of commercial enterprises and utilities
- foreign currency movement limitations
- armed conflict

Anticipated legislation

It is not enough to respond to legislation that has been passed by a government. The key is to anticipate changes and to prepare to take full advantage of any opportunities, which may be of a temporary nature. For example, if rear seat belts are to become compulsory within 12 months of the legislation coming into force, then there is a substantial short-term opportunity to supply and fit existing cars which are presently without them.

Better still, companies should seek to influence legislation before it becomes law if it is likely to have a substantial impact on their business. Multi-nationals have the resources to do this themselves, smaller companies may need to collaborate with their competitors to have sufficient influence at an acceptable cost, and small businesses may have to rely on the efforts of their trade association.

Consumerism and pressure groups

These should be looked upon as opportunities, often creating new market segments. For example, the pressures against added salt, artificial colourings and additives in foods have created the opportunity for manufacturers to offer an alternative product range to complement their traditional lines.

Making future market forecasts

The analysis outlined above should provide a basis for making future market forecasts. This should be done for each market segment and for different geographical territories within each segment where appropriate. The aim should be to forecast:

* annual market growth in volume terms

* opportunities for real price increases

* pressure to reduce prices or to avoid further increases despite cost inflation

- shifts in the importance of different distribution channels
- any imbalance in capacity and demand within the sector
- likely changes in the nature and extent of competition
- opportunities to introduce specialised products
- availability of skilled people, raw materials and energy

Action summary

1. Analyse your business into market segments and geographical territories to understand better what you are achieving within the market place.

2. Collect tangible evidence about the size and nature of the market and the factors likely to influence it.

3. Identify external trends and likely developments, so that you swim with the tide of opportunity and not against it.

4. Channel resources, people and money into the most attractive market segments in terms of profit growth potential as far as possible.

5. Look out for new market segments emerging and respond to the opportunities quickly.

4 | HOW TO TAKE STOCK OF YOUR COMPANY'S PERFORMANCE

In business familiarity may breed complacency rather than contempt. There is a risk of complacency setting in when familiarity tempts us to stop observing what is going on around us and learning from current experience. Try a simple test. Describe the curtains in your bedroom. You are familiar with them, but how accurate is your recollection?

How accurate is your knowledge of your business? As management consultants, whenever we are asked to audit company performance for a client, we find the tangible evidence collected and analysed provides some surprises. Taking stock of your company performance requires more than quantitative analysis. It often requires perceptive and different analysis from what is done presently. Some examples follow, and whilst they smack of managerial naivety, each one occurred in a well known company.

Customer profitability

The manufacturing subsidiary of a luggage manufacturer analysed profitability by three product groups. Product profitability was measured both on a marginal basis, i.e. sales revenue less directly variable costs, and at the pre-tax level after an allocation of fixed costs to individual product groups. There were no significant differences in profitability amongst the product groups.

A sales analysis showed that one customer accounted for 30 per cent of total sales, and was particularly demanding. Product-development costs were significantly higher to produce new own-label designs regularly for this customer, distribution was more expensive and customer liaison was particularly demanding. No other customer accounted for more than 5 per cent of total sales.

A customer profitability analysis was done for the six largest customers, and where indirect costs were significantly different from the average, such as external packaging and labelling, individual estimates were made for serving each customer. The results were surprising. The estimated profitability of the major customer was 1.6 per cent on sales, compared with over 6 per cent for the subsidiary as a whole. As the product life of the items produced for the major customer was short, it was decided to improve margins by tougher price negotiations for each new product line to be introduced.

For a business where any customer accounts for more than 10 per cent of sales, customer profitability should be measured at intervals and management action taken where appropriate.

Product costs

An electronics component manufacturer sold primarily customised circuits, but a quarter of the sales value was in standard circuits. As major mass manufacturers entered the market, the price of standard circuits fell from $7.25 to $2.89. The company responded by selling at market prices in the belief that at least some contribution was being made to central overheads.

When actual marginal costs were calculated for the standard products, based on direct material and labour costs, it was discovered that the marginal cost of production, excluding overheads, exceeding the selling price significantly. Evaluation showed there was no scope to produce standard circuits at an acceptable cost without becoming a mass manufacturer, and, as this was unattractive, the decision was taken belatedly to withdraw from the standard circuit business. Whenever sales prices are to be reduced significantly, accurate and relevant product costs information must be available as the basis for making decisions.

Total cost impact

The paper-manufacturing subsidiary of a group sold over 80 per cent of output to another subsidiary, for conversion into finished products. The pricing policy was on an 'arm's length' basis and the actual prices were marginally lower than competitors'. The paper-manufacturing plant was old and the business made only a small profit. In reality, however, the group was suffering a loss because the wastage and downtime suffered by the converting subsidiary was substantially greater with the in-house paper supply compared with competitive supplies. As a result of detailed evaluation it was decided to terminate paper-manufacturing and to buy all paper supplies.

There are occasions when a subsidiary or division pursues its own 'best interest' that this is not in keeping with the general group benefit.

Business appraisal

There is no doubt that outsiders are likely to produce a more challenging audit of a business, because they will bring a fresh perspective, though one need not necessarily use management consultants. Subsidiaries in a group could take stock of each other's business. Alternatively a non-executive director could be asked to do the analysis, and he would gain a valuable insight into the business by doing it.

Taking stock of a business cannot be done effectively in isolation. It needs doing by comparing the business with the leading competitors in each market segment and geographical territories.

The appraisal of a business needs to be comprehensive and should include:

- management
- product and services
- technology and innovation
- manufacturing
- marketing and selling
- distribution
- quality assurance and customer care
- financial performance
- likely competition

Each aspect will be covered in turn. The questions listed below have been designed to produce answers which will give a penetrating insight into a business. The purpose of this appraisal is to prompt action throughout the business at every level.

Management

- How strategic are board members and senior managers in their outlook?
- How market-orientated are people?
- How much customer contact do board members have?
- How much personal accountability to achieve results, rather than simply do a job, exists?

- How effective are internal meetings?
- Are operating decisions delegated sufficiently?
- What significant experimentation and innovation have taken place?
- Would a non-executive chairman or directors be helpful?
- Does the organisation structure help or hinder?
- Is management-development sufficient and effective?
- How constructive are employee and trade-union relations?
- Is outstanding achievement sufficiently rewarded?
- Is there sufficient functional expertise in each department?
- Are managers sufficiently qualified, where qualifications are appropriate?
- Is there sufficient management experience with first-class previous employers?
- Which additional expertise would be beneficial to have within the company, e.g. treasury management, graphic design, etc?

Once an appraisal of the management has been done, efforts should be made to maintain the objectivity. A non-executive chairman and directors are commonplace amongst quoted companies and those seeking a stock-exchange listing. Their use is much less widespread amongst subsidiary companies, but it is growing. It is not necessary to have someone outside the group as a non-executive. A main board director could act as non-executive chairman to ensure that sufficient breadth and objectivity of outlook exists.

Unquoted companies with no intention of seeking a stock-exchange listing, including family businesses, could benefit from a 'non-executive' input, though not necessarily someone appointed as a director. For example, the partner from the audit and accountancy firm will be unable to become a director because of the auditing role, but perhaps could provide a valuable input at board meetings. Alternatively a local lawyer or a self-employed management consultant may be suitable as a non-executive director.

Taking stock of a business cannot be done effectively in isolation

Products and services

These need to be appraised primarily from the standpoint of the market place and customer, then reviewed in terms of internal considerations such as research, development, manufacturing and profitability.

- Are there any gaps in the range which should be filled?

- Should the range be pruned?

- Are there any niche markets we should concentrate on?

- How can the product or service design be made more attractive to customers?

- How does the product or service compare with the competition for quality, reliability, benefits and features?

- How can we enhance the attractiveness of the product by improving the packaging and presentation?

- What can be done to create repeat business and to improve customer loyalty?

- How do price and discounts compare with competition?

- What scope is there for value analysis and cost reduction?

- Is there any opportunity to introduce a maintenance contract?

There can be no excuse for not having an up-to-date and in-depth knowledge of competitors. Superficial analysis is insufficient. Detailed factual information is essential. For example, when appraising product packaging and presentation it is important not only to have samples of competitive products but to have seen them displayed at the point of sale. Equally, totally different products should be examined to seek ideas.

Technology and innovation

- What percentage of sales revenue is spent on research and development each year?

- Is research and development focused sufficiently on market-place opportunities?

- Are research or development projects evaluated commercially before authorisation?

- What links exist with universities and other research organisations?

- Which new products or services have been introduced in each of the last 5 years and with what success?

- Which new technology skills are likely to become important to the business (e.g. biotechnology)?

- Is patent and trade-mark protection sufficient, or excessive?
- What should be done to retain technologists and to attract new staff?

Manufacturing

- How do product costs compare with competitors'?
- Is the product specification unnecessarily high or unacceptably low in some respects?
- What would we need to become the lowest cost producer?
- How does the use of new technology, techniques and materials compare with competitors'?
- What make *v.* buy options should be evaluated?
- What surplus capacity and bottlenecks exist?
- What is being done to manage energy costs?
- How do sources of supply, procurement methods and inventory management compare with our competitors'?
- What use is made of value analysis and quality circles?

Manufacturing is admittedly sometimes a difficult area in which to make detailed comparisons with competitors. Nonetheless it needs to be done. Employees joining from competitors can be a useful source of information, and some job applicants freely volunteer valuable information about their present employer during interviews.

Marketing and selling

- How well known is the brand name compared to competitors' brand names?
- How is the brand perceived by customers and non-customers?

- What promotional methods are used?

- What is the effectiveness of advertising and promotion efforts?

- What sales presentation and quotation techniques are used?

- What are the sources of new business?

- What incentives are provided to sales staff, distributors and agents?

- What awards for quality, design or service have been won? How are these publicised?

- What editorial coverage is obtained in the national, local and trade press?

- What sponsorship is undertaken and how much does it cost?

- Who are the major customers? How is selling to major customers organised?

Quantitative measurement and analysis are essential. An external market-research company may be needed to carry out telephone or field interviewing to assess brand awareness and perception. A major housebuilder engaged a market-research company to confirm that prospective customers perceived the builder's houses to be the best for quality, an opinion based on the builder's own detailed and factual comparison of similar houses built by competitors. The results came as a shock. Another builder came out on top for quality. The first builder had not succeeded in getting the quality message across, even though the firm had won more quality awards than any other competitor.

The value of advertising should be measured in terms of enquiries and orders wherever possible. Equally the results of exhibitions should be assessed in terms of enquiries, orders and renewed contacts with existing customers.

Some businesses are simply not aware of where new business comes from. This knowledge is particularly important, however, for professional firms and service companies, where a personal recommendation may be influential in the choice of company to use.

Other professional firms and people may be an important source of new business and should be cultivated. For example, law firms are asked to suggest an accountancy firm, merchant banks are asked to suggest financial public-relations consultancies, and so on. Unless the original source of each new client is identified, there can be no analysis to highlight the productive avenues to develop for new business.

Incentives should be used to encourage selling efforts. Experiments should be tried and measured. For example, an extra commission may be offered to field sales staff for each new account opened during a short campaign, and the results achieved compared with the previous period, before deciding whether to continue the incentive.

Awards are important. The Minolta 7000 camera won a string of major awards during 1985, and these were featured heavily in press advertising. It was clear that anyone considering a camera in this price range should at least seriously consider the 7000. But it is not only worldwide brands winning major awards that are worthy of publicising. A garage which wins a Regional Service Award from the car manufacturer should feature it in its advertisements in the local press, as well as displaying the certificate prominently in the customer reception area.

Editorial coverage carries more authority and impact in some market sectors than even the best press advertising. It does need effort, however, to get free editorial coverage. Fortunately the trade press and local newspapers are hungry for features. Contracts won, installations completed, expansion plans, awards gained, senior managers joining the company, new products and services are all suitable subjects to gain editorial coverage.

Existing major customers, potential ones and non-customers should be evaluated in terms of their purchases from competitors. It is important to understand the competitive advantages and vulnerabilities in each case. Purchasing habits should be monitored continuously. For example, when a large customer begins to give a greater share of its custom to competitors or starts to deal with another competitor, this must be identified quickly and action taken.

Distribution

- Which distribution channels are growing or declining in importance?

- What percentage share does the company have of each distribution channel?

- Which new distribution channels are emerging?

- Which alternative delivery methods have been evaluated during the last 12 months?

- Which alternative packing methods have been evaluated during the last 12 months?

- How quickly are orders delivered?

- Does the speed of delivery win or lose business for the company?

- What percentage of orders are part-delivered because of stock shortages?

- What is the value of goods damaged during delivery?

- What is the value of lost sales caused by stock shortages?

- What is the cost of distribution as a percentage of sales?

In some companies, even in well managed ones, distribution is the poor relation. It is seen simply as shipping goods instead of an important extension of the sales effort and customer care.

Quality assurance and customer care

- What measurable standards of quality assurance and customer care are set?

- What standards of quality assurance and customer care are achieved?

- How are staff trained and involved in quality assurance and customer care?

- What are the levels of customer complaints and warranty claims?

- How are complaints dealt with, and how quickly?

- What standards are set for responding to repair and maintenance requests?

- How are visitors greeted?

Customer care is an attitude of mind. Often the cost of outstanding service is not a penny more than a casual approach. The way guests are treated on arrival at a hotel is a good example. In some hotels the reception staff appears bored and uninterested, but when staying at Le Manoir aux Quat Saisons recently we were greeted with a single word, 'Welcome', and a smile. It was effective, for the hotel had clearly thought about how to greet people.

Measurement of the achievement of customer care is essential. For example, delay by switchboards in answering telephone calls is inexcusable. Whenever phoning your own office, check how long it takes for the telephone to be answered. Some companies which depend on telephone ordering set demanding and measurable standards for the speed of answering telephone calls, and one temporary help company supplying office staff aims to ensure that any telephone is not allowed to ring more than twice before it is answered.

Financial performance

Key measures and comparisons of performance include:

- return on sales

- return on investment

- earnings per share growth

- cash generation

- capital investment

Other comparisons which may be relevant include:

- sales per employee
- added value per employee
- profit per employee
- sales per square metre
- average remuneration per employee
- stock turn
- debtor payment period
- creditor payment period

The aim is to compare financial performance with that of competitors. If a competitor is achieving significantly better results, it is important to understand the reasons so that positive action may be taken.

Likely competition

Simply to take stock of company performance in relation to existing competition may be short-sighted. It may be important, or essential, to consider emerging or likely competition resulting from:

- new products, e.g. the introduction of the compact disc competing with the traditional long-playing record
- price break-throughs, e.g. the falling cost of video cameras is bringing increasing competition to the more expensive photographic camera
- different strategies, e.g. companies setting out to sell a wide range of related financial services to personal customers rather than one such specialised service as mortgages
- collaborative ventures, e.g. the collaboration between Honda of Japan and Rover of the United Kingdom to produce separate ranges of cars using some common development

Simply to take stock of company performance in relation to existing competition may be short-sighted

- take-overs, e.g. the impact of several major take-overs in the UK retail trade during the mid-eighties
- new entrants, e.g. the entry of Amstrad into the personal computer market

To summarise the situation of the company it may be helpful to map the competitive strength of subsidiaries, or product groups within a subsidiary, against the prospects for profitable growth (see Figure 2). The diameter of the circle shows the size of the business in each product area. The information in each sector indicates what the approach might be. This kind of mapping does not produce answers, but it can be a useful tool for showing the present status of product groups within a subsidiary or of subsidiaries within a group.

FIGURE 2. GROWTH PROSPECTS *v* COMPETITIVE STRENGTH ANALYSIS

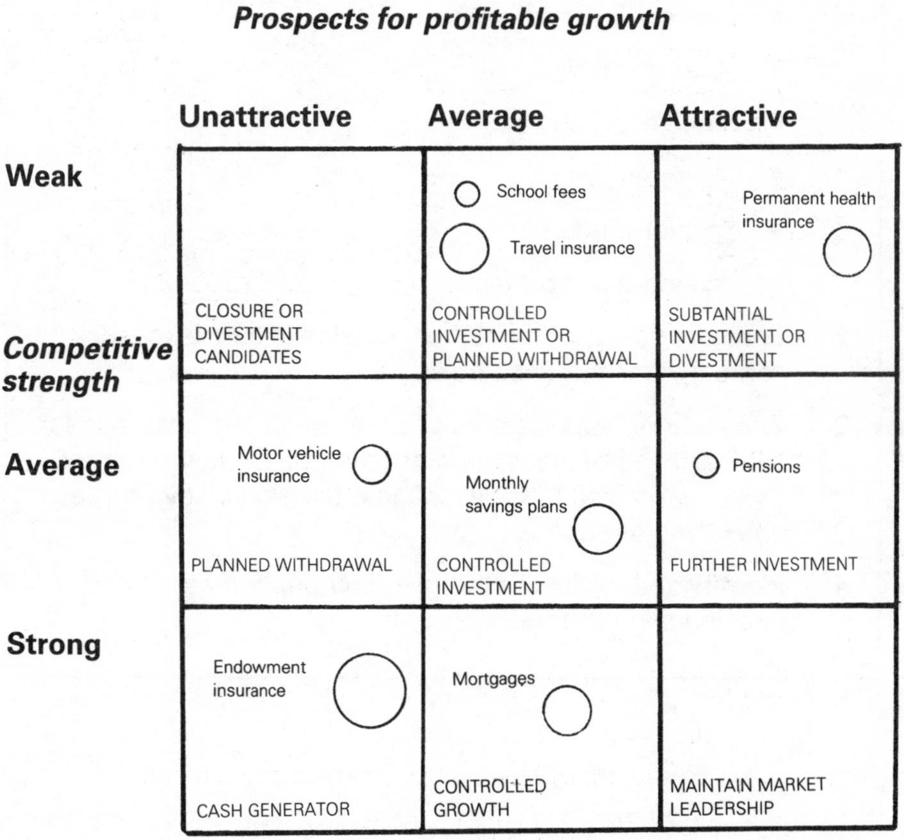

Prospects for profitable growth

	Unattractive	Average	Attractive
Weak		◯ School fees ◯ Travel insurance	Permanent health insurance ◯
Competitive strength	CLOSURE OR DIVESTMENT CANDIDATES	CONTROLLED INVESTMENT OR PLANNED WITHDRAWAL	SUBTANTIAL INVESTMENT OR DIVESTMENT
Average	Motor vehicle insurance ◯	Monthly savings plans ◯	◯ Pensions
	PLANNED WITHDRAWAL	CONTROLLED INVESTMENT	FURTHER INVESTMENT
Strong	Endowment insurance ◯	Mortgages ◯	
	CASH GENERATOR	CONTROLLED GROWTH	MAINTAIN MARKET LEADERSHIP

(for a financial services company)

Action summary

1. Measure performance quantitatively wherever possible, and compare it with competitors in terms of:

   - management

   - products and services

   - technology and innovation

   - manufacturing

   - marketing and selling

   - distribution

   - customer care

   - financial performance

2. Consider using someone from outside to help take stock of company performance objectively.

3. Consider the appointment of a non-executive chairman for subsidiary companies and unquoted ones, as well as for those listed on a stock exchange, to help achieve more objectivity of outlook.

4. Identify and evaluate emerging competition as well as existing competitors.

5 | HOW TO DEVELOP A VISION TO ENSURE SUCCESS

Every business should have a vision. It should be communicated to people. They should be committed to it, and it should motivate and inspire them. The vision should be written down, *on a single sheet of paper*, to help achieve these aims.

No business is too small to have a vision. Visions are not just appropriate to multi-national companies setting out to create worldwide brand names for their products. A specialist foodshop may have its own vision – to become the leading shop of its kind in the town or city perhaps.

Businesses do succeed without a written vision, sometimes spectacularly so. But the articulation of a vision and a commitment to achieving it will enhance and accelerate the achievement substantially.

The nature of the vision statement

A vision is not to be confused with a statement of financial goals. An effective vision statement combines the following ingredients:

* the broad commercial rationale, direction and priorities
* philosophy, policies and values

- qualitative goals to be achieved

- financial performance, in broad terms

- intentions on the future ownership of the business

Some further comment and illustrations may be helpful to give an insight into what is required.

Commercial rationale, direction and priorities

The aim should be to describe the commercial focus of the business. Some examples are:

- To become one of the leading suppliers of microprocessor-based building-management systems. To become one of the market leaders in the UK. To develop the business internationally by appointing overseas distributors, concentrating on the USA, Germany and France initially.

- To be recognised as the most outstanding management consultancy operating in the UK in the areas of corporate strategy, corporate finance, acquisitions and divestment.

- To create a restaurant group consisting of separate, nationwide chains of theme restaurants, incorporating the latest in audio and video entertainment technology. Central kitchens, incorporating the latest developments in food preparation, will be used where appropriate.

- To become one of the market leaders in the provision of a wide range of financial services and advice to wealthier individuals by developing a network of offices in the main towns and cities within the South East region during the medium term, and subsequently nationwide.

The above examples are not put forward as models to be copied, since a vision is necessarily subjective. Each of the above provides focus, describes the rationale and priorities where appropriate, and reflects the degree of ambition of the management team.

Philosophy, policies and values

The purpose should be to describe features which are to become central to the way the business is developed. Once again, these can only be illustrations rather than recommendations:

- Maximum accountability will be given to subsidiary companies, and head office staff will be kept to an absolute minimum.

- Wherever possible, each member of staff will have the opportunity to earn a significant performance-related bonus as part of total income.

- Equity ownership will be encouraged as much as possible amongst all employees.

- All products will be manufactured by outside suppliers to our own specification. These should be more original, perform better and be no more expensive than competitive products.

- Suppliers will be paid strictly on time in return for the keenest possible net prices.

- Peripheral services will be subcontracted to outside specialists wherever possible.

Qualitative goals

These focus the attention of the entire staff on the crucial areas for business success. Some examples are:

- Our snacks will reach the consumer in the freshest possible condition, and will be seen by our customers to be better than our competitors'.

- Incoming telephone calls will be answered by the second ring, because our business comes entirely by telephone.

- As patent agents, we will continue to adopt the latest technology to ensure that our patent record monitoring is as error-free as possible.

- Health and nutritional value will be key features of the specification and preparation methods for our food products.

- Our own label branded products will be perceived by consumers to compare favourably in quality and price with the leading manufacturers' competitive products.

Financial performance

Some examples which might be included in a vision statement are:

- The aim is to achieve a return of X per cent on capital employed by 1989.

- Y per cent of group profits before tax should be generated in the USA and Z per cent in the Far East by 1991.

- We will achieve a pre-tax profit of more than £500,000 within 3 years.

- We will double earnings per share within the next 5 years.

Future ownership

The vision will be affected by the nature or size of the business. Some examples are:

- We will obtain a stock market quotation within 3 years.

- The aim is to sell the business by 1990.

- At least three additional equity partners should be introduced within the next 5 years.

- Any business which is not expected to achieve the required return on investment within 3 years will be divested.

The horizon of a vision statement should be at least as far away as the medium term. In other words, one would not expect it to be rewritten every year.

How to start developing a vision

There are several effective ways to start developing a vision of success. Possible starting points include:

- finding out what senior executives think the vision is (the internal approach)

- finding out how people outside view the company (the external approach)

- asking a series of questions to identify the potential of the business (the questioning approach)

- defining what you want the company to become regardless of the present situation or the difficulties (the quantum jump approach)

Since some people find it difficult to start creating a vision, each of these will be considered in turn.

The internal approach

It is surprising just how many senior people simply do not have a vision for the business other than an assumed natural evolution along the present course. In some instances this will be entirely appropriate, but in other cases it is likely to be totally inadequate. For example, a loss-making subsidiary company having a vision which amounts to a recipe for 'more of the same' is almost certain to be unsatisfactory. Yet this is allowed to happen in some companies for too long before an acceptable vision is created.

It is highly revealing to ask the chief executive and each member of the executive committee to write down their vision of the business now and the vision it needs to have. The differences between people's perceptions are likely to be substantial. This approach is likely to demonstrate the need to create and to commit the business to a suitable vision for success.

The external approach

Some companies commission public-relations or market-research specialists to find out how outsiders perceive the company as a starting point to develop a suitable vision for success. In some cases the findings come as a shock to the company. Their belief that the company is perceived to be outstanding and only needs to maintain the present level of performance may be quite incorrect.

If this approach is to be adopted, the outside specialists should interview a wide cross-section of people, including:

- present customers
- former customers
- non-customers
- suppliers
- bankers
- auditors
- lawyers
- stockbrokers
- media people
- industry specialists

As with the internal approach, this method is likely to establish the need for a more relevant vision to achieve success.

The differences between people's perceptions are likely to be substantial

The questioning approach

The starting point comes from taking stock of company performance relative to competitors, as described in an earlier chapter. Then one should answer questions along the following lines.

- Which market segments and geographic territories is it possible to become market leaders in?

- Which ones should we minimise our future investment in?

- Which ones should we exit from or enter?

Supplementary questions which may be helpful include:

- What strengths and natural advantages do we have which should be capitalised upon more? For example, we make regular deliveries to every major chain of do-it-yourself retail shops and superstores. Could they not be used to supply additional product ranges?

- Are there any fundamental weaknesses or vulnerabilities we must overcome? For example, are training resources sufficient to ensure that the staff of our distributors are adequately trained in installation and maintenance of our products?

- What are our principal assets and how can we benefit more from them? For example, could the reputation of the brand name be used to launch a successful mail-order business.

- How can we achieve a quantum jump in results from our present activities? Could it be done, for example, by concentrating selling efforts to win major customers of nationwide retail chains?

- What obstacles are holding us back? How shall we overcome them? For example, our reputation for poor quality and reliability is losing us our market share and a drive to recover it must be launched.

The answers to these questions do not create the vision. They are likely to indicate just how much can be achieved, however, and to provide a basis for writing a vision statement.

The quantum jump approach

This approach deliberately sets out to ignore any shortcomings in present performance and likely obstacles to future success. In consequence, it is an arbitrary approach, requiring total commitment. Its strength is that it can galvanise people to take the action needed to achieve spectacular success.

Basically it has to come from the chief executive of the business, who has to demand truly outstanding corporate success from his team and motivate them to achieve it. For example, he may have a vision to:

- quadruple profits within 3 years
- become the market leader despite having only a small market share today
- enter a particular market segment and become market leader within 5 years
- start a company and become listed on the stock market within 5 years
- become the leading airline company in Europe in terms of passenger care

For any vision to be achieved, particularly one demanding high performance, it is not enough to write it down. The chief executive and every member of his executive committee need to:

- very much want the vision to become a reality
- *believe it will happen*
- be totally committed to make it happen
- not let any setback deter them
- communicate their belief and commitment to others

The question of ownership

The future ownership of the business should be considered as part of developing a vision. Ownership is too important an issue to be left to chance.

Different types of businesses require different considerations. So the following will be considered separately:

- companies listed on a stock exchange
- unquoted companies
- professional partnerships

Listed companies

Recent experience in different countries has demonstrated that virtually no company is sufficiently large to be protected from the possibility of being taken over. Equally statistics have proved that usually it is too late to start a take-over defence on the receipt of an unwanted bid. A spirited defence may obtain a higher bid for the shareholders or encourage a more acceptable company to make a counter-bid, but the outcome is still likely to be that the company is taken over.

The best defence against the threat of take-over, and even this cannot guarantee success, is to achieve outstanding results. The starting point for doing this is the appropriate vision. Companies are often taken over because the acquirer believes he can improve performance or realise under-utilised assets. If this opportunity is denied to potential bidders, then the likelihood of a take-over will be much reduced.

In addition to the defence against an unwelcome take-over bid, the board of a listed company should address other questions concerning ownership, including:

- Should we obtain a listing on stock exchanges in one or more other countries?

- Should we spin off part of our business by obtaining a separate stock-exchange listing for it and retaining an equity stake?

- Should we hive off our property portfolio into a separate company?

- Should we sell certain businesses or encourage management buy-outs because they no longer fit into our vision?

- Why do we continue to hold on to minority equity stakes in other companies?

- Should we set out to find a suitable company to merge with?

- Should we buy some of our own shares if legislation permits?

It is possible that any cash realised would be better invested in the mainstream business.

Unquoted companies

People managing unquoted companies, particularly family-owned businesses, tend to give little thought to the various options available for future ownership. Retaining the business to hand it over to the next generation of the family may have emotional appeal, but it may not be the most sensible course.

The options which should be considered include:

- Preparing the business to sell it for an attractive price.

- Inviting a financial institution to purchase a minority equity stake. This could provide either some cash for the shareholders or money to invest in the business by creating additional shares, or a combination of the two.

- Buying back some of the existing shares by the company, in countries where this is permitted.

- Capitalising some of the reserves to create fully paid up preference shares, which could be sold to financial institutions without affecting equity control at all.

- Creating a trust to own some of the shares.

- Selling and leasing back freehold property to realise extra cash to invest in the business, rather than seeking additional equity investment.

- Providing an incentive to the next generation of family management by allowing them to buy deferred ordinary shares with, say, neither dividend nor voting rights for 10 years, at a minimal valuation.

- Developing the company to obtain a quotation for the shares to realise some cash for shareholders and to establish a realistic market value for the shares.

- Merging with another company to accelerate the ability to obtain a stock-market quotation.

Whilst the present ownership situation may be the most suitable one, it is important that the owners of an unquoted company consider the available options and build the preferred one into their vision for the future. Specialist legal and taxation advice is essential to evaluate the possible options to ensure that any action to be taken is tax-efficient.

Professional partnerships

The question of ownership, size and management are closely connected. Questions connected with future ownership which should be asked within a professional partnership include:

- Is the firm large enough to have the range of specialist services the clients want?
- If not, should we seek a merger with a compatible firm?
- Are the partners getting old and the firm beginning to lose vitality?
- Are people being made equity partners young enough?
- Should our recruitment policy be to accept only people with the potential ability to become a partner?
- Should we attempt to sell the business for cash?
- Should we obtain a limited liability status if and when this becomes available?
- Should we obtain a stock-exchange listing if this is permitted?

The need for multiple visions

It is not enough for a group of companies to have a corporate vision for the whole business. People within each subsidiary or division need a vision for their own business to motivate and inspire them. Additionally, each function of a business may well benefit from having a separate vision. For example, the vision for a manufacturing department may be:

- to become the lowest cost producer for a given product specification

- to establish a lead over competitors by developing the latest process technology

- to seek the maximum possible asset utilisation compatible with profitability by continuous shift operation

- to purchase supporting production services where appropriate in order to concentrate on the production process

The vision for a marketing department may be:

- to create global brands to give customers maximum value by becoming the lowest cost producer from economies of scale

- to devise products capable of premium pricing to afford substantial and sustained marketing and sales promotion

- to use outside creative specialists when necessary to ensure the best results

Financial goals

People differ, and rightly so, in the extent to which they incorporate financial goals as part of a vision statement. Too many financial goals should be avoided. The choice of financial goals should differ for various types of business.

Companies listed on a stock exchange

The key goal should be:

- continued and uninterrupted growth . . .

- in earnings per share . . .

- throughout the medium to long term . . .

- which compares favourably with competitors and comparable companies

This is so important that it is essential for people working in listed companies and their subsidiaries to understand the reasoning behind this and just what is encompassed.

The earnings per share is the key profitability goal for a listed company because it is the profit after taxation earned on each ordinary share, which embraces:

- the pre-tax profit made by the company, after paying the interest on bank borrowings, which reflects the effectiveness of cash management

- minus the corporation tax payable, which reflects the expertise of tax management

- the effectiveness of raising additional finance, because issuing more shares means the earnings have to be divided among the increased number of shares

- the effect of issuing shares to make acquisitions, and the impact this has on the earnings per share.

So you can see that earnings per share reflect not just pre-tax profits, but cash management, taxation, fund-raising and acquisition policy.

Investors seek predictability in corporate performance even though ordinary shares are inherently a risk investment. Companies alternating good years with satisfactory or even poor ones are significantly less highly rated in terms of their share price, since people look for substantial improvement without setbacks over the medium to long term to give them confidence in the shares. Real growth means that the results should outpace inflation. Additionally, the growth should be better than competitors' and comparable companies' to justify a higher share price.

Subsidiary companies

Earnings per share is an inappropriate measure for a subsidiary company. The group board should translate the corporate earnings per share into goals for each subsidiary in terms of:

- the percentage return on the total investment in the business
- the returns to be achieved from new projects and acquisitions
- the amount of cash to be generated

Unquoted companies

Some companies set out to pay the minimum amount of tax the rules allow. Many unquoted companies under-perform because the owners already enjoy an attractive standard of living and have no more ambition. For any unquoted company with a vision to have a stock-market quotation in their shares within the next 3 to 5 years, however, its performance goals should already anticipate the requirements of a listed company.

Too many unquoted companies do not pay enough attention to cash management, yet the owners are usually reluctant to finance growth by injecting cash themselves. The growing and ambitious unquoted company should concentrate on cash management for just this reason.

Professional partnerships

The principal source of finance for most partnerships is a bank overdraft or loan. Too often, as a result of poor cash management, partners' drawings are limited by having to leave in the business a significant part of their profit share to provide finance.

The financial goal for a partnership should not simply be to maximise the drawings for each existing equity partner. The aim should be to provide an attractive standard of living for the present partners and enable the firm to promote talented people to equity partnership whenever they deserve it.

In conclusion

The writing of a vision statement acts as a catalyst for success. It is equally valuable for a partnership wishing to be recognised as the leading firm of lawyers in its own town as it is for an advertising agency seeking to become the largest and most respected in the world.

Action summary

1. Write a vision for your business, using only one sheet of paper.

2. Consider the questions of ownership and size as part of the vision for future success.

3. Set no more than two or three key financial goals as part of the vision.

4. Demand a total commitment from each member of the executive committee to make it happen. *Then it will happen.*

6 HOW TO OVERCOME OBSTACLES TO SUCCESS

External obstacles tend to be much more obvious to people than the internal ones existing within their own business. For example, many computer manufacturers are likely to view IBM as more of an obstacle to their achieving market leadership than their own deficiencies.

It can be difficult to see the obvious when you are too familiar with the situation in your own company. An example concerning redundant equipment illustrates this point. A new engineering division director was appointed to a major chemical plant operation and was faced with an immediate obstacle of a shortage of floorspace. He found space was being occupied by equipment which had been little used for years. He sold the unwanted items and released the space required as well. What is more, it was correctly regarded as profit because the accountants had written off the value of the plant several years before. There is a strong likelihood that you will find redundant equipment or stock which should be disposed of, if you set out especially to look for it in your own business.

The key point is, however, that obstacles can be turned into opportunities regardless of whether these are external or internal ones. The first step is to identify the obstacle. In the case of internal obstacles, these have often been unwittingly self-imposed. The biggest barrier to overcoming them may well be internal politics. Internal obstacles which affect corporate success must not be tolerated.

Sometimes people are well aware of an obstacle, but are unwilling to tackle it. The distribution director had served a dairy products company for almost 35 years since joining them straight from university. Eighteen months previously he had suffered a serious stroke, which left him partially disabled and bad-tempered, but he had returned to work. He began to criticise his deputy, a competent man, because he saw him as a threat.

Out of misplaced loyalty, the managing director did nothing about the situation until the deputy resigned and left the company. He was reluctant to retire the distribution director because the company had been his life. Finally the director's wife was approached about the situation. She said that she desperately wanted her husband to retire immediately but could not persuade him to request it. Needless to say, retirement on generous terms quickly took place. The delay need not have happened.

Unwittingly self-imposed

Internal obstacles

One of the most effective ways to identify internal obstacles is to bring in someone from outside the business to examine what goes on. For example, as an alternative to using a management consultant, it could be a non-executive director, an audit partner from the accountancy firm, someone from another subsidiary, or even another businessman.

Internal obstacles often fall into the following categories:

- people
- organisation structure
- rewards and incentives
- cash management
- expense levels
- time management

Examples of each category will be described in turn.

People

One of the most common obstacles is a reluctance to deal promptly with inadequate performance by a key person. Counselling, support, training and any other help which will remedy the situation must be organised quickly. If this does not work, then the person must be removed without delay, humanely and generously.

It is usually a totally misplaced sense of loyalty to create a job for the person who has been removed. Unless a suitable vacancy is available, then it is much better that the person should leave and rebuild his career in another company immediately.

It has to be said, too, that chief executives are as likely as anyone else to delay in dealing with this difficult problem.

Organisation structure

This really is a self-imposed obstacle to success, which often amounts to shooting oneself in the foot. Some examples illustrate the point.

One group of companies is structured into medium-sized profit centres to encourage accountability. It was decided that it would be sensible to have a central purchasing operation to buy common items for the operating companies. The chief executive decided that it should become a profit centre, so a margin was added to all purchases to cover the cost of the operation and to provide a profit. Quite soon operating companies began to purchase for themselves again as they objected to an 'internal profit' being charged to them by the central purchasing division. The good idea was going wrong. Only when making a profit from purchasing was dropped did the benefits of group purchasing occur.

A major drinks company was organised into product divisions in each country. This meant that they had several salesmen calling on each customer. Eventually a major reorganisation was carried out to overcome this situation, but only as a result of bringing in outside advisers to overcome the resistance of the existing divisional management. They knew that in a reorganisation of this kind there would be losers as well as winners in personal career terms.

Rewards and incentives

Salary scales and levels must be reviewed regularly to check that they are in line with market changes, particularly where there is a shortage of skilled people generally. Otherwise not only will it be difficult to attract suitable people to join, but existing staff are likely to leave. The cost of replacing an employee is substantial.

Investing in shares is a risky business. Shareholder reward in terms of share price and dividend levels depends on business performance, so it is equitable that a significant part of the annual income of the executive board members of a business should depend on the results achieved. Up to 25 per cent, or possibly more, of executives' income should be earned in this way.

Most people seem to believe they can devise incentive schemes as well as any expert, but many of the schemes in existence do not bear this out. An incentive scheme should focus management action on the desired result. Yet there are bonus schemes for subsidiary companies, where banking is centralised by the group, based on pre-tax profit achievement without any notional interest charged on the funds invested in the business. There is no incentive in this case for the managers to minimise the utilisation of cash.

Where directors are rewarded by a percentage share of group profits, this may encourage people to make acquisitions even when the result is a reduction in earnings per share. If the key result for a board of directors is to achieve outstanding and sustained growth in earnings per share, then there is a strong argument for linking their annual bonus to actual performance in this respect.

Too many companies use incentive schemes for sales people slavishly, with little imagination or even flexibility. For example, a percentage bonus on all sales is the bluntest of incentives. There should be a basic level of sales to be achieved without qualifying for any bonus in return for receiving a basic salary, allowing a significantly larger percentage bonus to be paid on additional sales to provide stronger incentives.

Incentive schemes for salesmen need to be more refined, however, to focus the sales effort in the most beneficial way. Schemes could include, for example, added incentives for opening new accounts and for sales of high-margin products. Equally, part of the total incentive bonuses paid to salesmen should be used for short campaigns, perhaps adding emphasis to a new product launch or responding to increased competition in certain product areas.

A professional partnership decided to give all fee earners other than equity partners a half-yearly bonus based on fees billed. This decision had a number of unexpected side-effects, including:

- The more senior people could earn larger bonuses by concentrating on their personal billing rather than for their whole team of fee-earners.

- Fee-earners generally were reluctant to take on non-fee-earning work which would benefit the business, because it reduced their earning ability.

- Some people held back interim and final billing of work when they would not achieve a bonus so that their bonus prospects for the next period would be improved.

The key is that an incentive scheme should:

- focus effort on the most important result to be achieved

- whilst not encouraging or enabling people to benefit by working contrary to the best interests of the business

Cash management

One example of poor cash management is widespread amongst professional partnerships and unquoted companies; namely, indequate cash collection. Examples include:

- A failure to ask for an initial payment with the order, particularly when early payments have to be made to other companies on behalf of the client.

- A lack of agreement with the customer or client at the outset to accept interim billing. Some professional firms take on projects lasting for longer than a year and do not send out an interim invoice.

- An unnecessary delay in sending out the invoice when the job has been completed, which is inexcusable and amounts to giving the customer extended free credit.

- Not having a prompt and systematic approach to collecting overdue payments from customers and clients.

Expense levels

An important part of a vision for success is to become the lowest cost producer. This does not mean simply achieving the lowest cost for the production process. Increasingly, in modern business, a substantial part of total costs are overheads.

Value analysis should be used to tackle overhead cost levels as well as production costs. Some companies are simply too tolerant of levels of expense. The questions to be asked of indirect departments should include:

- What would happen if we abolished the department?

- If that is clearly not possible, what is the minimum size of department which is acceptable?

- Should the work be done within operating companies rather than at head office?

- Conversely, should the work be done centrally rather than in operating companies?

- Should we purchase some or all of the service externally?

Time management

People really do allow work to become an obstacle to achievement. Many people are aware that Pareto's Law applies to inventory management, namely that 10 per cent or 20 per cent of the number of different lines of stock are likely to make up 80 per cent to 90 per cent of the total value of inventory held. The same 10/90 or 20/80 rule applies to a lot of management work.

For many directors, executives and managers 10–20 per cent of what they do contributes 80 – 90 per cent of the results achieved. Worse still, some people are so busy doing routine work that they do not make the time to do the important 10–20 per cent of their job.

The situation in a profitable unquoted tableware manufacturing company illustrates the point. Sales and profits had grown during each of the previous 5 years, but a significant trend was emerging. The product range had grown sharply and the average order value had declined in real terms. The managing director knew that the key to success was to pursue large retail chains as customers, whereas presently the sales force sold only to smaller customers. He was correct in his assessment that only he was likely to win business from potential major customers, but the internal obstacle was that during the previous 2 years he had allowed himself to devote his time almost entirely to sorting out production-control problems in the factory. Having recognised the obstacle, with the help of an outsider, he saw the obvious solution. He recruited an experienced production controller, who not surprisingly did the job better than he did, and was able to devote 2 days a week to winning new customers.

External obstacles

Winning companies do not merely identify the existing obstacles to success, they anticipate what are likely to be the requirements for future success. External obstacles to success which need to be anticipated and overcome include:

- technology
- legislation
- the likely impact of take-overs on customers, suppliers and competitors
- economic prospects
- consumerism
- new competitors
- social change
- political factors
- changing distribution channels

The attitude must be that obstacles which are anticipated sufficiently early can most readily be turned into opportunities, so there is a need to be continuously watching emerging trends in the outside world. Some examples illustrate these points.

- The early recognition of the changing demand from typists to word-processing operators provided a temporary staff agency with the opportunity to develop the necessary capability before the lack of it became an obstacle to success.

- A company which recognises a continuing depression in the home market may amend the vision to pursue overseas markets or to diversify into other market segments at home.

The key to overcoming external obstacles is to avoid them by continually reviewing what will become the essential ingredients for success. The business then may stay ahead of competitors or amend its vision accordingly.

Action summary

1. Identify and tackle internal obstacles vigorously.

2. Bring someone from outside into the business if there is resistance to change.

3. Anticipate external obstacles to success by monitoring trends, and turn them into opportunities.

4. Identify surplus assets and stock, then sell them to realise cash and to release space.

7 HOW TO DEVELOP MAJOR ALTERNATIVES

To make a quantum jump in achievement often requires that at least one major alternative approach is pursued. Simply improving what exists already is unlikely to be sufficient, because in many market segments in various countries it appears that competition is increasing more than growth in the market.

Nonetheless there is a real danger of people becoming channelled into set ways of doing things and only considering minor variations. This can be seen across the whole spectrum of different types and sizes of business: it might be described accurately as 'furrow management', because it is comfortable to keep on ploughing the same management furrow.

Brainstorming, lateral thinking and innovative approaches need to be encouraged throughout the business. The aim should be to identify options and alternatives across the whole spectrum of possibilities.

Consider the range of possibilities for major business development. These include:

- organic growth
- licensing and royalty deals
- franchising your own business
- minority equity stakes
- joint ventures and consortia

COMMON-SENSE BUSINESS STRATEGY

- mergers and demergers
- majority equity stakes
- take-overs and reverse take-overs

Each one will be considered in turn.

To identify options and alternatives across the whole spectrum of possibilities

Organic growth

If there is such a thing as a panacea for business success, then it is effective organic growth, which means developing the business internally. People should be encouraged continuously to come up with new ideas and variations on existing ones for products, market segments and sales opportunities.

In a lot of technical industries collaboration with universities and research establishments can be valuable. Universities around the world are working to exploit the commercial opportunities arising from their research work, often in the form of a company established in conjunction with commercial businesses.

Within the avenue of organic growth there are major alternatives to be considered. The important thing is to list the range of possible alternatives. Valuable sales opportunities may come from a variety of possibilities, including:

- Should we promote a limited edition of our product? Many car manufacturers do this, so why should companies in other market sectors not do the same? It can be a way of countering competition or boosting sales in the short term, by offering customers an attractive price, without unduly undermining normal pricing policy.

- Should we focus on major customers? This may require setting up a small, high-level sales team and recognising that results are likely to come more slowly than selling to much smaller customers. With increasing domination of many retail sectors by large chains, however, effective selling to major customers is likely to become increasingly important.

- Should we offer to create different products for selected major customers? One approach is to create a different model exclusively for a major customer to sell by offering to customers an attractive 'special promotion' price. An alternative would be to offer to create a product range or design especially for a major customer to offer as an own-label product. By taking this kind of initiative, it may be possible to develop a different type of outlet for the product from what exists already.

- Should we transform a specialist service into a branded standard product? There are many possibilities, such as car-servicing, picture-framing, computer-maintenance, the supply and maintenance of plants to decorate business premises, and the provision of linen to restaurants. Some of the most attractive opportunities come from ideas which are not being pursued yet in your market sector or region of the country.

- Should we adopt a low-cost, no frills approach? Some of the biggest success stories in retailing during the last 10 years have followed this route. The key to success is to be bold enough to be an early entrant into your chosen field and achieve a lead over your competitors.

- Should we concentrate more on product design and point-of-sales presentation? Customers are prepared to pay premium prices for well designed products. Equally, attractive point-of-sale presentation can have a dramatic impact on sales. The use of in-house staff can lead to a tired and dated look in design. The use of freelance designers and specialist product-design agencies maybe more expensive, but could be well worth trying.

The above examples are merely indicative of many more alternatives which may achieve a quantum jump for you. The purpose of illustrating a few examples is to persuade you to create your own range of alternatives. One innovative approach is to look at what is done in totally different industries or countries and then to consider how to adapt this to your own situation.

Licensing and royalty deals

A quick and relatively inexpensive opportunity can be found by becoming an exclusive licensee or distributor for a territory. There are opportunities in many industries, and not just technical ones, to join forces with, say, a US or Japanese company. There are situations where a young company is concentrating on its home market and does not have the resources to push overseas sales.

One company found a US manufacturer of a patented table decoration for restaurants which would complement its own product range, and secured an exclusive UK distribution licence, with an option for several other European countries, subject to meeting an agreed minimum sales level. The arrangement has succeeded so well that a joint manufacturing company is being set up to serve the European market.

Having identified licensing and royalty deals as a possible opportunity, you must seek them out and not sit back to wait for them to come to you. The trade press, visiting trade exhibitions, overseas visits, chambers of commerce, trade associations, and government agencies may help to identify opportunities.

Franchising

Franchising is the arrangement whereby a company enables people to run their own business, using a proven format and the support of the franchisor. Companies with some franchised outlets include McDonalds, the hamburger chain, and Prontaprint, the printing service company. In a successful franchise operation, the customer should not be able to tell whether a particular branch is owned or franchised, because the quality and presentation will be identical.

The development of franchising in America during the last 20 years has been dramatic. It now accounts for a significant proportion of all business activity there. The Americans have demonstrated that the only limitation to franchising products and services is the bounds of imagination. The pace of franchising elsewhere is accelerating. The problem is that many businessmen outside the USA never stop to even consider the opportunity which franchising their business to other people may bring them.

The large hamburger chains have many thousands of outlets

around the world, including a significant proportion of franchised ones. Names such as McDonalds, Burger King and Wimpy are known in many countries. On a lesser scale, however, outstanding theme restaurants such as The Hard Rock Café in London and Browns in Oxford could be a very attractive franchise opportunity. People are to be seen queuing on the pavement outside both regularly, which indicates their popularity.

The fundamental requirement for a franchising operation is an original concept, capable of widespread duplication given the necessary support from the franchisor. Large companies and small businessmen alike should stop to consider whether they are sitting on an attractive franchising opportunity. This could provide a way to pursue an opportunity quickly with a much lower financing need.

Minority equity stakes

Minority equity stakes require careful consideration. There should be a definite purpose for committing funds to make a minority equity investment. As the years pass, the reason for making the original minority investment may no longer apply; so companies should regularly review their minority investments to decide whether or not they should be realised and the proceeds invested in the mainstream business.

A minority equity stake in an unquoted company merits caution as well as careful consideration. There may be a requirement that any shares to be sold must be offered for sale to other shareholders first, which could well mean there is little opportunity to realise the true worth of the investment. Even if not restricted in this way, there may be a lack of prospective investors wishing to pay a realistic price for a minority stake. Worse still, with a minority stake in an unquoted company, if the business runs into difficulties you may have the ability and desire to help, only to find your offer of assistance is rejected.

When purchasing a minority equity stake in an unquoted company, make sure that the investigation is done as thoroughly as if you are making an outright acquisition. Additionally, you should obtain board representation and recognise that a non-executive director needs to do more than simply attend board meetings to be effective. To make a contribution as a non-executive director requires up to 2 or 3 working days a month, otherwise it is nothing more than a monitoring role.

At the outset it is desirable to negotiate the terms and duration of an option to gain majority control or outright ownership, or both of these in stages, within an acceptable time. In some countries local indigenisation decrees require that foreign investors cannot obtain majority control of any company in certain industrial sectors. This does not necessarily mean that the opportunity should be rejected prematurely. It may well be possible to have management control and an acceptable remittance of dividends, whilst having only a substantial minority equity investment.

Joint ventures and consortia

There are numerous examples where joint ventures and consortia projects have proved to be a considerable disappointment. They are too important, however, to dismiss out of hand.

Joint ventures and consortia can be as valuable to the small business as they have proved to be for multi-nationals. The terms joint venture and consortia should not necessarily imply the formation of a separate company, with all the necessary formalities. For example, a number of small accountancy firms in a city may wish to collaborate to provide improved and more cost effective professional training for staff. Small farmers may wish to form a marketing company to distribute their products at an acceptable level of overhead cost.

On a larger scale oil, mineral exploration and construction companies have demonstrated that joint ventures and consortia projects can be successful. The approach should be that it is better to have a slice of an attractive cake, rather than none at all, if one cannot have the whole cake.

Joint ventures and consortia projects should be considered where one or more of the following situations exist:

- The range of skills required is beyond the scope of your company: for example, a construction project with a substantial proportion of specialist underwater work.

- The size of the project or particular contract is too large in relation to your own resources.

- The investment is necessarily speculative. For example, it may be desirable to have a stake in the exploration of several oilfields rather than to risk the total investment in one field.

The key to the success of joint ventures or consortia begins with the choice of partners. It is important that the management styles and people are compatible. For example, an entrepreneurial company able to make decisions quickly may find it frustrating to work in a joint venture with a large company where decisions require approval from a head office located in another country.

Another important ingredient for the success of a joint venture or consortia deal is for the project to have its own management team. In this way the partners should look upon themselves as investors and not indulge in management by interference. Alternatively, one of the partners may be given management accountability and the others regard themselves as investors. 'Management by interference', however, must be avoided at all costs.

Even if a project is set up as a limited liability company, which has a perpetual life, various options should be considered from time to time:

- Should our stake be sold to another partner?

- Should we buy out the others, or seek to get majority control?

- Does it make sense to sell off the whole entity to a third party or to seek a stock-market quotation?

- Should the entity be terminated because the original opportunity or purpose has passed?

Mergers and demergers

One could debate whether or not there really is such a thing as a merger. Putting this aside, mergers may be particularly relevant for smaller companies and professional partnerships. It may be desirable to merge in order to be of sufficient size to provide the range of services customers and clients expect. Alternatively, for companies it may be an attractive way to accelerate entry to the stock market or to overcome a problem caused by the lack of management succession in a family business. Conversely, the demerger of part of a group by a stock market flotation, a sale to a third party or a management buy-out may make commercial sense and provide a more attractive return by reinvesting the funds realised.

Majority equity stakes

There should be a positive reason for acquiring a majority stake in a business, as opposed to outright purchase. One reason may be to provide motivation for continuing management of a business following acquisition. If so, you are recommended to secure an option at the outset to purchase the remainder of the equity by means of a pre-determined formula within a given period of time.

Another sound reason for having a minority equity investor may be in a foreign country in which it is desirable to have a local company as a partner. If necessary, you should find a local company to invest along with you, particularly where it is not appropriate for the previous owners to retain a minority equity stake.

Once again, the key thing is to identify the possible options and evaluate them objectively.

Take-overs and reverse take-overs

Many acquisitions turn out to be less successful than expected. They are certainly not all panaceas. However, acquisitions are an important alternative to achieving a quantum jump. Progress equivalent to several years' organic growth may be made by one acquisition. The starting point should not be an acquisition policy but a carefully thought out commercial rationale and direction as part of a vision for success. As acquisitions are so important, and a potential minefield, the next chapter will focus on how to make successful acquisitions.

Major alternatives within functions

This chapter has concentrated on identifying major alternatives for corporate development. These should be supported by each functional manager identifying the main options available.

For example, alternatives within a manufacturing function could include:

- setting up an overseas manufacturing operation

- building a factory where there are attractive government incentives to help create jobs

- making a major investment in robotics as part of a commitment to become the lowest cost producer

- switching some production to outside manufacture to your own specification

- subcontracting supporting services such as canteen facilities
- pioneering a no-strike, single trade union agreement

It does not matter whether or not these examples are relevant for you. They illustrate the need to identify alternatives across the whole spectrum in every facet of the business. Encouraging individual managers to do this provides management-development benefits from a form of continuing action learning.

Action summary

1. Identify and evaluate the major alternatives for corporate development across the whole spectrum of possibilities.

2. Consider organic growth, licensing and royalty deals, franchising your business, minority equity stakes, joint ventures and consortia projects, mergers and demergers, major equity stakes, and take-overs and reverse take-overs.

3. Encourage each functional manager to identify and evaluate the major alternatives possible within his own function.

8 HOW TO MAKE SUCCESSFUL ACQUISITIONS

Common sense tends to go out of the window with acquisitions. Egomania and emotion may well replace it. What is required, however, is strategic common sense.

Opportunism is an important part of acquisition success. There are times when a business is likely to be more receptive or more vulnerable to a take-over approach because of the temporary situation that exists. Success demands being prepared for opportunities, and not being forced into taking risky short-cuts.

Making a successful acquisition requires the following stages:

- a sound commercial rationale, direction and priorities as part of a vision for success

- an acquisition profile to define relevant companies

- an active search programme to speed up finding suitable companies to acquire

- winning the support of the target company, whether it is a quoted or unquoted business

- an investigation of target companies

- a valuation of the worth to you of the company to be acquired

- negotiation skills to make a winning bid

- effective post-acquisition management

The previous chapters have described how to develop a vision for success and to identify the alternatives for corporate development. So it will be assumed in this chapter that acquisition is the relevant alternative to be pursued. Each stage of making a successful acquisition will be described.

Commercial rationale and direction

Some types of acquisition are inherently more likely to succeed than others. Diversification by acquisition can prove to be particularly risky. To help ensure acquisition success it is important to explore these issues.

Sound reasons for acquisition include:

- increasing market share, subject to anti-monopoly or anti-trust regulations in the country concerned

- extending the product range, primarily involving the same distribution channels and selling to the same countries

- acquiring more production capacity or facilities

- protecting a key source of supply, one whose acquisition by a competitor would be damaging

- acquiring a number of sales outlets, e.g. high-street retail shops or out-of-town superstores, which may be in short supply, in order to expand a nationwide chain

- obtaining particular expertise, e.g. a biotechnology research team

- offering the client a comprehensive range of services to provide 'one-stop shopping'

- obtaining outstanding top management by a reverse take-over

Diversification is not always readily apparent. People tend to think of diversification in terms of tangibles such as different products or production technology. Types of diversification which may not be obvious but are very real include:

- selling via a different distribution channel, e.g. direct-response advertising is markedly different from selling the same products to wholesalers

- selling to major customers rather than to many small customers, because quite different people and skills are likely to be needed

- marketing branded consumer products rather than industrial products

- managing a service company rather than a manufacturing business

Diversification is not always readily apparent

- doing business in a different country, e.g. where customer attitudes, legislation, distribution channels, or the infrastructure are quite different.

An important feature for acquisition success where diversification is concerned is for the acquirer to be able to contribute an asset or skill which will add significantly to the success of the acquired company. Examples include:

- providing access to major customers and overseas distributors of the acquirer

- offering cost-effective central services such as purchasing power, physical distribution, or sales invoicing and credit control

- supplying particular expertise which may be relevant, such as financial management, computer-aided design, environmental testing, etc.

- providing resources such as cash for expansion, additional production capacity, use of regional depots and sales offices, etc.

How to write an acquisition profile

Some managers find acquisitions an exciting distraction from every-day work. This is potentially dangerous. Time devoted to acquisitions is easily wasted, unless efforts are focused effectively. An acquisition profile is a sound way to minimise abortive efforts.

An acquisition profile should translate the commercial rationale of a vision for success into a meaningful description of the type of company required. Unless there are only a handful of companies worth acquiring, and they are easy to identify, an acquisition profile will provide a valuable focus to help the search for suitable target companies.

The acquisition profile should ideally be written on one side of a sheet of paper, and certainly on not more than two, and the elements it should cover include:

- a description of the business, and the products or the services required
- the maximum funds available to make a purchase
- the minimum profit and profitability required
- the location acceptable
- whether or not continuity of management is required
- whether or not a performance-related deal or 'earn-out' is sought
- the basis of valuation to be used to determine the maximum to be paid
- any key features for success

A written profile is so important for acquisition success in many situations that each item will be considered in turn.

Products or services

Broad descriptions of a market sector such as leisure or financial services are too vague. More precision is needed. For example, a suitable description might be:

> An insurance broking company serving wealthier private clients, with a bias towards the self-employed and small businesses. Pensions and tax-efficient investments should be a significant part of the business.

Maximum funds available

It is important to ensure that the funds available for acquisition are large enough to buy a suitable company. Small company acquisitions can be particularly risky. Success may be heavily dependent on the continued commitment of the present owners, and the fact that they are prepared to sign a lengthy service contract is no guarantee of their continued commitment.

The acquisition of a larger company, with senior and middle managers in addition to the owners, is likely to provide a more assured basis for success. In addition, the amount of time required to make an acquisition and to supervise it afterwards is virtually the same over a wide range of size of the company acquired.

Minimum profit and profitability

Any acquisition is likely to be a significant burden on the management team during the acquisition process and afterwards. It must be sound common sense to make sure that the potential profit opportunity likely to arise is commensurate with the management time spent. If not, it is better to invest the efforts into organic-growth projects. Setting a minimum level for the current amount of profit and the level of profitability to be achieved by an acquisition should ensure a sufficient return on the management time spent.

It must be recognised that the purchase of a company which is performing unsatisfactorily, is making a loss, or is in receivership, requires a totally different approach. A different and full-time chief executive should be installed as soon as the change of ownership takes place. Additionally there is a strong case for the new chief executive taking part in the investigation leading to the decision to buy the company. Otherwise there is a chance that he may subsequently suggest the company should never have been acquired. This kind of hindsight is of no benefit. Turning round a loss-making company requires quite different skills from managing a successful business, so it is advisable to choose someone as chief executive with proven experience of turn-round situations.

Location

The location of an acquisition is an important consideration. If considerable post-acquisition management and integration is likely to be needed, then travelling time can be an added burden.

If the intention is to create a nationwide chain of insurance brokers by acquiring one company, followed by rapid organic growth, then it may be considered important that the company to be acquired is located in the leading financial centre of the country. The existence of some regional offices may well be desirable, but not essential. Such considerations need to be thought through at this early stage of the acquisition process.

Continuity of management

In a successful business the impact of losing one or more key people should not be under-estimated. Their contribution to research or to winning new business may be difficult to replace quickly. On the other hand, if the existing management team is to continue, then it is essential that the management styles are compatible. Clashes are likely when a bureaucratically managed group acquires an entrepreneurial business which is run in an informal way.

Performance-related or 'earn-out' acquisitions

When people receive large capital sums as a result of the acquisition of an unquoted business, their commitment to the future success of the business is likely to decrease sharply. One method of countering this is to make a significant part of the purchase consideration dependent on future profit performance. Specialist tax advice should be obtained to ensure that these deferred purchase payments based on future profit performance are subject only to any capital gains tax which applies and not to penal rates of income tax.

If the period during which performance-related payments are

earned is too short, there is a risk that short-term profits will be pursued to the future detriment of the business. Conversely, it must be recognised that the ability to interfere with the business or to merge it with another one is restricted during the performance-related period.

Some performance-related acquisitions are based on profit-related payments for up to 7 years. In most circumstances, even with service companies, which are particularly dependent on key people, it is unlikely that a period of longer than 3 years, or at most 5 years, is appropriate.

Equally it is strongly recommended that an upper limit is set for performance-related payments, or there is a risk that people will be encouraged to maximise profits to obtain the largest possible deferred payments, at the expense of the continuing business. Performance-related payments should be based on pre-tax profits, rather than profits after tax. This means that the vendors do not receive additional payments for advantageous changes in tax legislation or as a result of tax expertise provided by the group leading to reduced taxation payable.

In the purchase contract to buy the company the basis of trading between the acquired company and the rest of the group needs to be set out. This includes the pricing policy for trading with other companies in the group, the cost of central services provided, any group overhead charge, and the interest cost of any financing provided by the group.

Performance-related acquisitions reduce the risk to the purchaser. If performance does not live up to expectations, then the total price of the acquisition will be lower. It would be wrong to give the impression, however, that these offer a guarantee of success. Vendors can only be expected to agree to a performance-related purchase when they are to continue managing the business. Equally, particular care must be taken in devising the incentives to be offered. Any subsequent disagreements, even if arising from a genuine misunderstanding, are likely to be damaging.

The basis of valuation

There is no right answer for the value of a business. The valuation must enable the enquirer to obtain the financial return required and reflect the commercial benefits to be gained. If this valuation is below the figure at which the company can be acquired, then it would be wrong to attempt to justify a higher purchase price in order to make an acquisition possible.

There are various methods which are appropriate for valuing a business. It is recommended, however, that two or more different methods are used to help decide the maximum amount to be paid.

The valuation methods most widely used include:

- The earnings multiple

- Return on capital employed

- Discounted cash flow analysis

- Asset backing

The valuation will still depend on the yardsticks of performance set by a particular company. A description of these methods is outside the scope of this book, although a chapter on the Valuation and Offer is included in the author's *Successful Acquisition of Unquoted Companies* available from Gower Publishing.

Features for success

The only practical assumption is that there are no perfect companies to be acquired. So it is likely to be counterproductive to produce a long list of essential features that would ensure success. It is much more realistic simply to highlight two or three key features essential or highly desirable for success.

For example, it may be highly desirable for a suitable insurance-broking company to have:

- well developed computer systems

- in-house tax expertise to advise clients

- a research capability to evaluate 'best-buy' products

Acquisition search

Common sense demands that you do everything possible to make success happen, and not simply wait for it to do so. This means an active acquisition search must be made.

Various avenues need to be pursued simultaneously to maximise the chance of acquisition success, particularly if the company to be acquired is likely to be an unquoted one. These include:

- making contact with merchant banks, stockbrokers, business brokers, major audit firms, receivers, and specialist management consultants to find out if they know of relevant companies available to purchase or interested to receive an approach

- using desk research, with the help of electronic data bases, market sector surveys and published directories

- advertising your requirements and replying to advertisements

- getting editorial coverage of your acquisition plans in the financial and trade press, provided the disclosure of your intentions will not be disadvantageous

- making reference to acquisition requirements in your annual report to shareholders

Winning support

The vision statement may be superb, the acquisition search may be first-class, but if you do not win the agreement of the target company, all of this is likely to come to nothing. With a quoted company, one can simply announce a bid without any discussion. The result may be a bitter fight and the target company may seek a white knight, a bidder of their choice, to rescue them from the unwelcome approach. With an unquoted company, however, if the vendors reject the approach, then that is the end of the matter, at least for the time being.

Consequently the proposition has to be sold successfully to the target company. In most situations it cannot be done effectively by writing, although people do sometimes rely on a letter, surprisingly enough. The preferred approach is to set up a meeting, or possibly a lunch, without indicating your wish to pursue an acquisition at the outset. Otherwise the invitation to meet may be rejected.

The person to be approached depends on the type of target company:

- for a company listed on a stock exchange – the chairman or chief executive

- for a subsidiary company – the approach should be made at group level to avoid an unwarranted rejection by the subsidiary company management

- for an unquoted company – the controlling shareholder if there is one, who may not necessarily be either the chairman or the managing director; or an institutional shareholder if there is one

- for a professional partnership – the senior partner

Some companies use a third party to make the initial approach to a target company for one or more of the following reasons:

- to avoid disclosing their identity unless the target company is prepared to meet them to explore the possibilities of acquisition

- to sell the merits of the acquiring company and the benefits of the deal – perhaps important when acquiring in an overseas country or where the acquirer may be looked upon unfavourably by a target company

- to establish that a performance-related purchase will be accepted at the outset, if this is regarded as essential, to avoid wasting time

- to benefit from using full-time experts to handle one of the most crucial aspects of the whole acquisition process

Investigating the target company

'Let the buyer beware' is essential advice. Desk research is important, but it is not sufficient. Face to face discussions are needed. In the case of a contested bid for a company listed on a stock exchange, any discussions will be unwelcome, so the uncertainties are increased.

When the bid for a listed company arouses no acrimony, then every opportunity should be taken for discussion, whilst taking care to avoid a premature disclosure which would require an immediate announcement of the intention to bid. With an unquoted company, a thorough on-site investigation is necessary. Ideally this will be done before the purchase negotiations, although the vendors may insist that commercially sensitive information is not revealed until agreement of the purchase terms has been reached and the lawyers instructed to proceed towards legal completion.

The investigation of a target company should cover the relevant history, current performance and future prospects of the business. It must not be purely a financial investigation, but should cover the whole business, including:

- marketing and sales

- research and development

- manufacturing

- distribution

- key people and personnel information

- finance

A key aspect to be established is that the management styles of the companies are likely to be compatible. Successful acquisitions are primarily about people.

Valuation

This is no right answer for the value of a business, since the value to the bidder and what the shareholders are prepared to accept have to be reconciled. Depending on negotiating skills and any scarcity or rarity value (because of a shortage of suitable companies in a particular market sector), the actual price paid may be significantly different from what might be considered to be the market worth of the company.

A starting point for valuing a business is the most recent set of audited accounts. However, these need to be adjusted to take into account:

- the impact of different accounting policies, e.g. different depreciation rates

- the effect of any prior year adjustments or extraordinary items

- any unrepresentative circumstances, e.g. excessive directors' salaries and pension contributions

Budgets, management accounts and the most recent year-end forecasts for the current financial year should be examined. Then the bidder should make his own assessment of the likely results for the current year. Most bidders will then wish to produce profit and loss and cash-flow projections for the next 3 years, based on their plans for the business.

The price to be paid by the bidder has to be acceptable to the shareholders of the vendor's business and meet his own criteria in terms of:

- the price-earnings multiple to be paid

- the pre-tax return on investment to be achieved from the acquisition

- the generation of cash in terms either of the number of years to achieve a cash pay back of the investment or the discounted cash-flow rates of return to be achieved, if this measure is used by the bidder

COMMON-SENSE BUSINESS STRATEGY

- the percentage of assets backing obtained relative to the
  purchase price

With bids for a listed company, a significant premium will generally
have to be paid over the current market share price to gain control. A
premium of a third over the current share price is not unusual, unless
the anticipation of a bid has already caused a significant increase in the
share price.

In contrast, an unquoted company tends to command a lower
rating than a comparable quoted company. A discount of 20 per cent
may apply, but this could be significantly higher or lower, depending
on the scarcity of either buyers or sellers in a particular sector. In
addition, professional fees are substantially lower when making
unquoted acquisitions. So common sense suggests that unquoted
companies are a better financial bargain, provided a suitable business
can be bought.

Negotiation and winning bids

Valuation skills are important, but negotiation expertise and bid
tactics determine whether or not the acquisition will succeed.
Negotiation skills are crucial for unquoted acquisition success. The
purchase price to be paid should be the last item to be agreed, but a
sensible price cannot be arrived at until the following items have been
agreed:

- any lump-sum termination payments or pension payments for
  directors being asked to retire (this approach may be
  tax-efficient, but any payments must be regarded as part of the
  purchase price)

- the terms of the service contracts for those directors continuing
  with the company and any other other key executives

- the purchase of any significant assets of the company by
  individual shareholders at below market value

- any conditions that the vendors insist upon and which may affect profits

If the purchase price is agreed first and then these issues are negotiated, it will mean the total cost of the acquisition is likely to be increased.

Auctions for unquoted companies should be avoided. Before negotiating, it should be established that there are no discussions in progress with other bidders. If the vendors attempt to insist on negotiating with other people simultaneously, you should ask for a short exclusive option period during which you will either complete negotiations or terminate your interest. If this is not acceptable to the vendors, you may wish to consider the possibility of withdrawing until other bidders have negotiated rather than take part in an auction. Obviously winning control of a contested bid such as this is crucial not only to the price to be paid but to whether or not a deal will be negotiated at all.

Take-over bids for listed companies can be made without prior consultation. You should consider first, however, the benefits of making an agreed bid which has the support of the directors. If their shareholdings are substantial, a winning bid may be virtually assured at the outset. If the bid is not an agreed one, then tactics are vital for a winning bid. The arguments for the bid must be convincing to institutional investors, private shareholders and the media, so communication and public relations are important.

Whether you are making quoted or unquoted acquisitions, outside advice from full-time experts should be sought. It cannot make sense to reject specialist help on such an important issue, which happens only infrequently in most companies. This applies even more for vendors of family businesses and unquoted companies, as it is unlikely they will have any previous experience of selling a company.

Post-acquisition management

Post-acquisition management really starts before the company has even been acquired. The investigation stage is an important opportunity to learn about the business, and first impressions will also be formed about the management of the company during the negotiation stage. This can prove to be either a help or a hindrance later, so investigation and negotiation should be carried out with this in mind.

A lot of preparatory work needs to be done before legal ownership is transferred to ensure a successful start to post-acquisition management. It is listed in the following pages.

Informing staff

A personal note to members of staff is insufficient. Their working lives are being changed to some extent, and rumours are likely to abound.

Meetings with people should take place during the first day of new ownership to announce the acquisition and invite questions. Considerable care should be taken to avoid giving rash assurances. For example, you cannot responsibly *guarantee* that there will be no redundancies within the next few months, even if none are envisaged.

It is desirable to rehearse the likely questions and the answers to be given before these staff meetings take place. If different locations are used, then a common briefing is necessary to ensure a consistent message is put across. This could take the form of preliminary meeting, a written briefing or a video-cassette to be shown to people.

A tour of offices and factories by the directors of the acquiring company is a good idea. People appreciate a real interest being taken in their jobs and the contributions they make to the success of the company.

Informing customers and suppliers

A huge number of customers may be suddenly acquired, so that an immediate visit to them all is impossible. A customer-contact

Meetings with people should take place during the first day of the new ownership

programme does need to be ready for launch before ownership is transferred, and there may be some customers who are sufficiently important for an early visit by a director to be made. Even the smallest customer should receive a word-processed letter promptly announcing the change of ownership, unless there is a particular reason for wishing to play down the acquisition, which is difficult to imagine. People will find out quickly anyway, and it is better to receive a courtesy letter than to be told by a competitor's salesman.

Suppliers deserve the courtesy of a prompt letter announcing the acquisition, and some of them may be sufficiently important to warrant an early visit. Once again, preparation in advance is needed, and this is an aspect which people tend to overlook.

Financial control

Financial control must be achieved immediately following an acquisition. Depending upon the particular circumstances, this may include:

- changing the banking arrangements

- setting new authority limits for cheque-signing

- formal approval of capital expenditure and certain items of revenue expense over a certain sum

- approval for hiring additional staff in excess of agreed figures for the remainder of the current financial year, until properly authorised budgets are available for the next financial year

This may seem elementary advice. It is. Unfortunately it is not applied universally. One well known public company discovered during the annual audit that the managing director of a subsidiary acquired during the financial year, who had received over £10m for his own shareholding, had arranged for the lavish party he gave to several hundred staff as a personal thank you to be paid for by the company. Financial control must be achieved *immediately the acquisition is completed.*

Following an acquisition, group finance staff should resist the temptation to demand that uniform monthly management reporting procedures are installed immediately. In a company with established monthly reporting procedures a change in the reporting formats during the year is disruptive enough, but for an unquoted company, which is not used to producing monthly management accounts, substantial preparatory work is needed before meaningful figures can be produced.

Initially the first requirement should not be to demand that uniform monthly reporting is installed, regardless of the circumstances, but that the following essentials are immediately achieved:

- *accurate* monthly results are produced quickly, in whatever format is most appropriate

- reliable forecasts of year-end results are made and updated regularly

- cash-management procedures are effective and cash-flow forecasts are sufficiently accurate

General management

Even if the managing director of the acquired company has signed a lengthy service contract, there is a risk he will not like the new regime and leave. So a potential replacement should be available, and preferably this should be someone already working within that business. This may mean making an internal transfer of a suitable person at the outset to provide the necessary cover, even if a suitable vacancy has to be created to enable this to happen.

Where the acquired company is to be a separate subsidiary and the same management team are to continue managing the business, it is important that the person at group level responsible for the business should *make* time to learn about the business. Ignorance of the acquired company leaves post-acquisition management success too much to chance.

Action summary

1. Write an acquisition profile to translate your vision for success into a focused search for attractive target companies.

2. Carry out an active acquisition search programme to make successful acquisitions happen. It is not enough simply to find out which companies are known to be available to acquire.

3. Persuade the target company to merge with you. Seek an agreed bid for a listed company if possible.

4. Investigate the target company as thoroughly as possible before valuing the worth of the business to you.

5. Consider using specialist outside help for negotiation and managing the bid tactics.

6. Start preparing for post-acquisition success before legal completion and ensure financial control is secured immediately.

9 HOW TO TURN AROUND LOSS-MAKING COMPANIES

Urgent and decisive action is essential. In a loss-making business, as with a road-accident victim, the first step is to stop the bleeding.

This is obvious and common sense. Unfortunately, too often the response is indecision and procrastination. In one group with a turnover of over £1 billion analysis showed that the worst performing subsidiaries had produced a sizeable aggregate loss in each of the previous 2 years. These subsidiaries accounted for over a third of total group turnover, and the current year forecast showed little improvement for them; yet the group board displayed no sense of urgency to tackle the problem. Good results in the remainder of the group meant that performance was satisfactory, but it could have been much better.

Unless the chief executive of a loss-making company has a convincing plan to restore success as quickly as is possible in the particular circumstances which exist, he should be removed promptly. The problem is that people with a record of managing successful companies to achieve greater success often have no experience of turning round loss-making companies. The management style required is very different. In a successful company a newly appointed chief executive will take time before making significant changes, but in a turn-around situation the new person must make his impact felt from the first day.

The new chief executive needs to be full-time, and a substantial amount of overtime will be required initially. He will need the

. . . The new person must make his impact felt from the first day

support of an experienced financial manager. If one does not exist within the business, then someone should be provided immediately, on a temporary secondment from elsewhere within the group if necessary.

A programme is necessary to ensure that progress is achieved quickly. An outline programme could be:

Day 1 – Take financial control and make an impact.

Week 1 – Deal urgently with any cash-flow crisis which threatens survival.
– Assess the financial performance in broad terms.
– Initiate financial analysis as a basis for making short-term decisions.

      – Start to decide the level of initial cost reduction necessary.

Month 1 – Investigate each area of the business.
      – Decide the level of cost reduction required in each function.
      – Ask people to make specific recommendations to achieve the cost reduction required.
      – Make preparations for the headcount reductions needed.
      – Carry out the headcount reductions needed.

Month 2 – Initiate short-term profit-improvement projects.
      – Set a budget for the remainder of the financial year.

Month 3 – Begin to create the vision for future success.
      – Define major business-development projects to create an adequate return on funds invested.

The actual timing will depend upon the size and complexity of the business.

The first day

Urgency must be displayed at the outset. Financial control must be secured immediately. Initially, strict scrutiny will apply to:

- placing purchase orders
- signing cheques
- recruitment, including replacing people who leave
- foreign travel

An impact needs to be made. Some items of avoidable and non-essential expense should be terminated immediately. If it is damaging the business, someone will complain. Examples where immediate cost reduction should be made include:

- Personal expenses. Lavish meals, expensive hotels and first class travel should be replaced by a more modest approach. There should be no exception allowed. The chief executive must set a personal example.

- Temporary staff. All temporary staff should be terminated immediately unless they are revenue-earning or essential to serve the customer.

- Company cars. Cars should be replaced only when the cost of repair becomes unacceptable.

- Discretionary expenses. Plans for items such as re-equipping staff canteens, painting offices and other non-essential expenditure should be delayed.

The first week

If there is a cash-flow crisis threatening the survival of the business immediate action must be taken. This may include:

- Using senior managers and partners to collect overdue debts by telephone call or personal visit wherever appropriate, concentrating on large amounts which can be received quickly.

- Negotiations with bankers and others to secure additional finance or an increased overdraft facility.

- Negotiations with tax authorities to avoid legal action for overdue payments and to agree a phased payment schedule, provided that penal interest rates are not charged.

- Paying only those invoices necessary to avoid legal action and to ensure continuity of essential supplies and services.

- Seeking extended credit terms from major suppliers wherever appropriate.

Much of this action may only be needed temporarily.

The rest of the first week should be spent searching out the reasons for making a loss.

Sometimes the financial analysis is not available to highlight the extent of the problem. In one turn-around situation, in the silicon-chip industry, only out-of-date costs were available, the current actual product costs not being known. Falling prices caused by rapid technological change and surplus capacity elsewhere in the industry meant that some products were being sold for less than the standard product cost, on the assumption that at least a reasonable marginal

If there is a cash-flow crisis threatening the survival of the business, immediate action must be taken

profit was being made. An urgent and necessarily approximate marginal cost analysis showed that the market price for the best selling product had fallen below marginal cost. Every unit of this product which was sold increased the loss, and the more that were sold the bigger became the loss. Drastic and urgent action had to be taken.

Other problems may include a shortage of orders, inaccurate contract-cost estimating, inefficient production, costly subcontract work and excessive overhead levels. A swift decision on the immediate level of cost reduction needs to be made.

The first month

The remainder of the first month should be spent assessing each aspect of the business at first hand. By the end of the month, preparation for any headcount reductions required should have been made. If the law requires a minimum period of notice to be given before redundancies can be made, then the need for urgency is even greater.

Sales

The sales department, rather than marketing, is the recommended starting point for examining the business, as it is closest to the customer. To find out the true sales situation, there is no substitute for accompanying salesmen on customer visits. One can quickly find out both customer reaction and sales effectiveness.

The next area to examine should be the sales-support functions, such as the sales office, estimating department and after-sales service. Aspects to be examined should include:

- What credit status checks are made on prospective customers and what is the level of bad debts?

- How accurate are product and contract cost estimates?

- How competitive are prices, quantity discounts and payment terms?

- What are the authority and basis for quoting non-standard prices?

- How quickly and professionally are quotations submitted?

- How quick is delivery? Are sales being lost because of long delivery periods?

- What is the level of out-of-stock situations?

- What is the level of complaints and warranty claims, and how well are they handled?

- How quickly and effectively are telephone calls and correspondence actioned?

Marketing

Marketing should be examined next. The knowledge gained from the sales operations should be of valuable help in assessing marketing effectiveness.

It is particularly easy for people to confuse work and results in marketing. Factual answers should be obtained to searching questions such as:

- How does the department measure its own effectiveness?

- What tangible results and contribution have been achieved?

- How is the effectiveness of advertising, exhibitions and other promotional activities measured?

- What is known in detail about the market and competition?

Manufacturing, distribution and administration should be examined next. Questions to be asked include the following.

Manufacturing

- How can we reduce product costs without additional capital expenditure?

- What is needed to reduce product costs significantly?

- How can reject and wastage levels be reduced?

- How can product quality and reliability be increased without additional cost?

- Which production bottlenecks need to be overcome?

- How can delivery times be shortened without additional facilities?

- What small outlays of expenditure would produce substantial profit improvement speedily?

- How can raw-material, work-in-progress and finished-goods stocks be reduced without prejudicing profitable sales opportunities?

- What surplus equipment and redundant stocks should be sold off?

Distribution

- How can distribution costs be reduced?

- How can deliveries be speeded up?

- What are the levels of damaged goods and items returned?

- How else can customer service be improved?

- How are peak-period requirements dealt with?

Administration

- What would happen if we stopped doing this task, or scrapped the whole department?

- Why is it done daily and not weekly, or weekly instead of monthly etc?

- Could it be done less expensively in another department or location?

- What jobs are being left undone, to the detriment of the business?

Research and development

Research and development is probably, but not necessarily, the last department to be examined. Questions to be asked include:

- What proportion of the total budget is spent on:
  - fundamental research?
  - new product development?
  - improvements to existing products?

- What is the status of each current project?

- What are the market, commercial and financial arguments for continuing each project?

- What projects are planned to start in the foreseeable future?

- What tangible results have come from the department in recent years, and what failures?

At the end of this review of the company the chief executive should decide upon the level of cost reduction to be achieved in each department. A common percentage cost reduction in each department may appear to be equitable, but it is almost certainly inappropriate.

Then the head of each function should be asked to make specific proposals for the people to be dismissed and other cost reductions to be made, for approval by the chief executive. Speed and confidentiality are important, as rumours and anxiety are inevitable.

The second month

Redundancies should be announced simultaneously across the whole company, for people need to be assured and to believe that further redundancies will be unnecessary. A second round of redundancies is likely to cause lasting damage to morale.

Department managers should submit concise written profit-improvement plans, for immediate implementation, and give an estimate of the effect on current-year profits.

Revised budgets should be prepared quickly for the remainder of the current year. The chief executive will need to review and approve each departmental budget to ensure that the level of achievement proposed is sufficiently demanding.

The financial analysis which has been done will allow the monthly sales figure required to be calculated to achieve a break-even position. Every manager must be aware of the figure and a target month agreed upon as the deadline for exceeding that figure.

It must be realised, however, that eliminating losses is only the first stage of a successful turn-around. The goal must be to achieve an adequate return on the total funds invested in the business. Eliminating losses is usually the easier and quicker task. Selecting a few key tasks to be done urgently, simply and outstandingly well is often sufficient to eliminate losses. To achieve a satisfactory return on investment in a turn-around situation may require major new initiatives to be taken, particularly if there is a surplus of capacity in the industrial sector.

The third month

By now the worst of the upheaval and disruption should be out of the way. No time must be lost in building future success. A vision statement should be written with the total commitment of the management team. Their major business-development projects should be identified, and personal accountabilities assigned, as the means of translating the vision into tangible achievement.

The vision statement and business-development projects need to be addressed before budget preparation for the next financial year is begun. The budget process should be particularly rigorous in order to provide a clearly thought-out operating plan for the coming financial year. The management team must realise that the agreed budget represents a collective cabinet commitment to achieve the profit and cash-flow budgets.

Two of the most valuable assets for the chief executive are enthusiasm and belief. He must exude them every day, however tough the going becomes. Gradually his belief and enthusiasm will be shared by the rest of the management team.

Action summary

1. Take control and make an impact on the first day.

2. Attack a cash-flow crisis during the first week.

3. Assess each department and decide the initial cost reduction required during the first month.

4. Carry out any headcount reduction needed during the second month.

5. Develop a vision for future success and define major business-development projects during the third month.

6. Recognise that approximate financial analysis done quickly is much more valuable than waiting for accurate figures to be produced.

10 HOW TO HOLD A STRATEGIC WORKSHOP

Strategic workshops are not new, but they are widely misunderstood and misused. When used effectively, they have proved to be dramatically successful in major groups, subsidiaries, divisions, family businesses and professional partnerships; and there is no reason why strategic workshops should not be just as effective in the public sector.

The divisional board of one company held what was referred to informally by those attending as an 'away-day' once a quarter. This was a more accurate description than a strategic workshop, which was what the chief executive believed it to be. The 'away-day' consisted of a discussion on the expected financial results for the current year, one or two guest speakers from outside the company, an up-date on what was happening elsewhere in the group, a discussion allowing people to bring up subjects of their choosing, and a good lunch. It was really nothing more than an opportunity for the management team to spend time together in a relaxing way.

Other examples are easy to find. Sometimes the only real difference is in the expense. A subsidiary of a food company held its annual strategic workshop in places such as Cannes and Marbella. Managers took their spouses with them and over half the time was given up to organised outings and social dinners. Productivity relative to cost was at an all-time low. If companies choose to reward their executives in this way, so be it. They still need strategic workshops.

Having illustrated what a strategic workshop isn't, let us describe what it is. Its purpose should be to:

- address issues of strategic importance to the business

- bring together the members of the executive committee, the board or other controlling body

- provide sufficient time for discussion, free from interruptions and matters of detail.

Since each subsidiary company or division of a group needs to have its own strategy, so strategic workshops are as applicable to them as at group level.

The benefits of strategic workshops

In addition to providing an effective means to develop strategies for success, there are other benefits to be gained. Sometimes these have been sufficiently important to a business to prompt the chief executive to hold a workshop.

The benefits of strategic workshops, some of them less obvious perhaps, include:

- developing the sense of collective cabinet accountability amongst the top-management team

- improving motivation, morale and team spirit

- an unusual opportunity for management development

- encouraging plain speaking

To get the most benefit out of strategic workshops it is necessary to have an insight into these aspects. So each benefit will be considered in turn.

Collective cabinet accountability

It is quite inadequate in any business for only the chief executive to be concerned with the success of the whole enterprise, whilst other directors or executive committee members concentrate on their own job and merely attend board or executive committee meetings. This situation occurs more widely than people may think.

Strategic workshops should be used to develop a sense of collective cabinet accountability amongst every member of the board or executive committee. This requires that each person is primarily concerned with the success of the business, and does not let 'doing his job' get in the way.

An actual example from a European hotel chain which occurred

. . . Developing the sense of collective cabinet accountability amongst the top-management team

some years ago illustrates this point well. The business was under-performing. The chief executive, with a very autocratic management style, had been removed, and the new chief executive happened to have a highly participative style.

When he arrived, morale amongst members of the executive committee was low. Based on his initial assessment, he decided to give the existing executive team the opportunity to prove themselves. They were looking to him, however, not only to provide the vision and commercial rationale for success, but to tell them what to do, which was the way his predecessor had worked. He rejected this completely. Instead he organised a series of three strategic workshops during a 4-month period in which he required his executive team to present him with their collective view of:

- a vision for success
- the commercial rationale and priorities needed
- the organisational changes required

This was done with a minimum of overt intervention or influence from him, but with the help of some telling questions for them to reflect upon. Quite deliberately, he used an outsider to chair the workshops and only attended himself from time to time to check on progress.

The outcome was an ambitious vision for the future, a rigorously thought through commercial rationale and set of priorities, and an organisation structure to overcome some of the problems which presently existed. His executives felt it was *their* strategy, which had his full support. Collective cabinet accountability has been achieved in full measure. The tangible success which has been achieved since then is nothing short of spectacular.

Improving motivation, morale and team spirit

These things are best improved when addressing some specific business purpose, rather than pursuing so-called classroom team-building exercises in isolation. What better way is there to create winning teams than when addressing issues which are crucial for the success of the teams' own business? An example from a well-known publishing house illustrates this point well.

The sales division and the distribution division were almost at loggerheads. Backbiting and sniping at each other were commonplace at different levels within the two divisions.

At their first strategic workshop, the chief executive decided that 'distribution' was an essential strategic issue to discuss. The discussion which followed was revealing and productive. It soon became clear to the divisional managers that they had not spent enough time communicating and collaborating with each other. They lacked sufficient understanding of each other's operation. Each one was doing some things which unknowingly aggravated the situation, even if only to increase the sense of frustration.

At the workshop, any bitching was promptly channelled into constructive and positive discussion. Mutual understanding was the priority. The chief executive then allocated members of the executive committee to one of two teams during the workshop. One was chaired by the distribution division director and the other by the sales division director.

Their task was separately to articulate a vision for an outstanding distribution facility and then to meet together to agree upon a shared vision. The next step was to have a brainstorming session to come up with ideas to help turn the vision into tangible reality as quickly as possible. The distribution division director was charged with developing an action plan in the weeks following the workshop in order to implement the vision.

Not only did a much improved distribution service result, but teamwork and morale were much improved.

A management-development opportunity

Strategic workshops offer a management-development opportunity which is too good to miss. In a strong management team every person thinks like a businessman first and foremost. Additionally, he contributes technical expertise, which may be research, production, marketing or whatever.

In some companies which have been dominated by either engineering or production, people have asked if it was being suggested that their technical expertise was no longer valuable or relevant. Absolutely not is the only answer, but it is not the complete answer. A high standard of engineering, for instance, cannot be allowed to remain a goal in itself. Engineering projects and standards have to be relevant to the market need, and affordable, given the level of pricing acceptable in the market place.

The real management development opportunity afforded by strategic workshops is illustrated by a specialist engineering company which made and sold a particular sub-assembly. The sales growth and profit achieved appeared sufficient to justify a quotation of the shares on the unlisted securities market of the UK Stock Exchange, but the sponsors who were approached to bring the company to the market were hesitant for two reasons. The company was virtually a one-product business and sold predominantly to one large customer. It was run by two brothers, one the chief executive and the other looking after finance and data-processing, although he was not a qualified accountant. There were several other directors, but they were really middle-management heads of department, with no equity in the company.

It was decided to use a series of strategic workshops within the space of a few months to lay the foundations for:

● reducing the one-product and one-customer dependence

● developing the other directors' ability to contribute to the business as a whole and to take a strategic approach towards their own departments

The initial reaction was understandable: namely, are we being criticised when the company has been demonstrably successful to date? Reassurances were given and accepted.

The outcome of the series of strategic workshops was commitment to several business-development projects to achieve the stated objectives. Each one was made the personal accountability of one of the 'non-family' directors as an essential part of their management development.

Once again the outcome is a definite success story. The company has progressed from the original goal of a quotation on the unlisted securities market to become a fully listed company of the Stock Exchange.

Encouraging plain speaking

This may seem a surprising benefit, and possibly an unnecessary one, to come from strategic workshops. As a management consultant, I am disappointed with the widespread lack of plain speaking even by some of the most senior executives and directors. There is a telling expression: if you really want to get your own back on your boss, always do exactly what he asks, without question.

Effective managers need to display courage, which includes the ability and commitment to:

- tackle unpleasant and difficult jobs without delay
- not to be discouraged by setbacks
- *say what one really believes and thinks*
- *ask the questions that get to the crux of a matter with the precision of a laser beam*

Somehow people are more ready to say exactly what they think during a strategic workshop than elsewhere, and it is something which should be demanded. Then it should be positively encouraged afterwards.

Arrangements

Successful strategic workshops don't just happen. They need careful planning as regards:

The widespread lack of plain speaking even by some of the most senior executives and directors

- location

- duration

- timing

- numbers attending

- agenda

- 'position papers'

- minute-taking

- outcome

- social aspects

Each of these will be considered in turn. As in so many aspects of business, it is giving sufficient attention to the important details that is the key to success.

Location

It is a false economy even to think of holding a strategic workshop on company premises. The location must ensure that interruptions and distractions are totally avoided. People should give themselves completely to the strategic workshop, forgetting about their jobs and families temporarily. So it is important to choose a location where people are not even tempted to call in at the office or to go home at night during the workshop.

There should be no telephone in the room where the workshop is to be held. Telephone messages should be kept to an absolute minimum and they should be held until the end of each working session.

If the workshop needs people to work in more than one group, then additional rooms should be available.

The flow and continuity of discussion should not be interrupted by tea and coffee breaks. Drinks should be delivered to the room for people to help themselves without creating an interruption.

A country-house hotel can provide a suitable venue for a strategic workshop. It offers the chance of some fresh air or a swim when a break is taken.

Meals must be efficiently organised. Long-winded and heavy lunches are to be avoided. A light, self-service and speedy buffet lunch is needed, to allow people to mingle and to continue discussing points informally where appropriate.

Duration

Experience has shown that between 1½ and 2 days for discussion is about right, with one addition. Participants should arrive in time for dinner on the preceding evening, to ensure that everyone will be present for a prompt start in the morning, which is essential. In addition, it provides an opportunity for the chief executive or senior partner to set the scene and to emphasise the importance of the issues to be addressed.

Any attempt to hold an 'away-day' should be rejected. It usually provides insufficient time for discussion and people need time to escape from daily matters and to concentrate on strategic issues.

A workshop which does not end by the second full working day is too long. It is difficult to sustain the level of debate and there is a real danger of anticlimax.

Timing

Obviously clashes with events such as budget-preparation deadlines and important trade exhibitions should be avoided. Even so, some businesses are understandably reluctant to have the whole executive committee absent at one time. So there is a strong case for getting together on either a Thursday or Friday evening and continuing to work through at least part of the weekend.

This is not a recipe for executive hardship. If people have to give up a weekend to take part in a strategic workshop, then they are likely to expect a great deal from it, which is all to the good. An effective strategic workshop will have a substantial influence on the future success of the business, so a working weekend is a small price to pay.

Numbers attending

There seems to be a real temptation to invite twenty or thirty people to attend a strategic workshop. This is nonsense. It is a totally misplaced sense of participation.

Attendance should be restricted to the chief executive and those reporting directly to him. Some harsh words or home truths may be said by anyone during the workshop, and rightly so if appropriate. There are times when someone may be criticising a particular senior manager, which means it is quite unacceptable for people from the next organisational level down to attend.

Experts should be brought in, where necessary. For example, if a senior manager has a valuable input to make to the discussions on a particular subject, then he should be invited to attend for just that item.

Those attending will wish to consult the managers reporting to them in preliminary discussions before the workshop, to the extent which is appropriate. Equally, they will wish to brief people afterwards on relevant aspects of the outcome of the workshop.

Agenda

The choice of items to be included and the order in which they are placed on the agenda are vital ingredients for the success of any strategic workshop. Any thought of including items left over from the last board or management meeting must be discarded, as must any idea to include a 'few quick items to get them out of the way'. Experience shows that these may eat up half a day of the precious time available. The agenda should consist only of:

- those items which are of the strategic importance to the future success of the business, arranged in an order which reflects their relative importance, as well as a sensible sequence in which to discuss them

If the most important item is placed last on the agenda, there is a danger that poor chairmanship may mean that the item is reached only just before the end of the workshop.

There is a natural tendency for people to want to include everything on the agenda, but this must not be allowed to happen. The danger is that most of the items will be aired but not resolved, simply leaving a sense of frustration amongst those present.

Whilst a rigid timetable is not appropriate, the chief executive should decide roughly how much time will be needed to deal adequately with each item. Then he should tailor the length of the agenda to suit the time available during the workshop. It is unlikely that much progress can be achieved on more than five or six items during one workshop. Occasionally some issues may be of such fundamental importance that there will be only two or three items on the agenda.

'Position papers'

Each item on the agenda of a strategic workshop needs to be properly introduced, otherwise a rambling, time-wasting and inconclusive discussion is likely to follow. At the very least the agenda should indicate alongside each item who is to introduce it. Better still, a concise 'position paper' should be distributed before the workshop to introduce each item on the agenda.

The position paper should in a concise way:

- remind people why the item is of strategic importance

- summarise the essential data needed for a meaningful discussion of the subject

- outline the various options available and factors to be considered

- indicate the type of outcome expected from the workshop, e.g.
  - to authorise expenditure, recruitment, or whatever
  - to approve a specific option
  - to select one or two options for further evaluation
  - to set terms of reference for a working party
  - to define a major business-development project

Minute-taking

Do not attempt to take minutes. It is likely to prove too embarrassing, and a record of who said what is irrelevant. So a secretary should not attend. It is only the outcome which is important.

Outcome

The outcome of a strategic workshop can be evaluated in terms of:

- decisions made
- major business-development projects authorised
- further analysis and evaluation to be done

These are best captured by using flip-charts and felt-tipped marker pens during the workshop. The flip-charts will then serve as the basis for producing a brief record of the action to be taken after the workshop.

Perhaps one of the best examples of the outcome of a strategic workshop came from an insurance company – a single sheet of A4 paper which described a handful of major business-development projects, together with the person accountable and the completion deadline for each one. That single sheet of paper was the catalyst for a substantial change in the direction, achievement and future prospects of the whole company.

Social aspects

Social aspects must not be allowed to detract from the outcome of a strategic workshop.

Alcohol should be kept to a minimum at lunchtime, and at dinner if work is to continue afterwards. A hangover next morning is totally unacceptable. There are some definite benefits from not working after dinner during a strategic workshop. People are unlikely to switch off anyway and providing time for informal discussion can be particularly valuable.

The attendance of spouses is an unwanted distraction. At most, allow them to attend to the final lunch, if you must.

Sightseeing is simply an unacceptable waste of time and detracts from an event of strategic importance to the future success of the business.

The dangers of strategic workshops

Strategic workshops sometimes become emotionally charged, which may well be healthy, and very occasionally they become explosive. In one instance, the managing director of a subsidiary company was receiving considerable criticism from his colleagues during a strategic workshop. There came a point when he walked out and did not return. Shortly afterwards he left the company. In another case, a director offered his resignation privately to the managing director at the end of a working session. Instances such as these happen only rarely, and perhaps the workshop only accelerated what would inevitably have happened anyway. Plain speaking is required, but the leadership of a strategic workshop should be such as to avoid unproductive outbursts.

Strategic workshops set up expectations amongst those attending, and this can be dangerous.

One company was run in an autocratic way by a chief executive and his finance director. Pressure was mounting from the other directors for a greater say in the direction of the business and important decisions. A strategic workshop was held. People left on a high note. A list of actions, admittedly mainly to analyse and to evaluate, had been agreed. It really amounted to nothing more than a cosmetic exercise. Six months later the analysis and evaluation had come to nothing. Expectations remained unfulfilled, and the sense of frustration was markedly greater.

During a strategic workshop the mood of the participants may become depressed when contentious problems are being aired without any acceptable solutions in sight for the moment. This happens quite often. The chairman must ensure that contentious and negative aspects are dealt with during the early part of workshop so that it ends on a high note.

A strategic workshop must be more than a talking shop. Decisions taken, business-development projects authorised and further action agreed are the required outcome. Otherwise any sense of increased motivation will soon wear off. What is worse, people are likely to approach the next workshop with a cynical attitude.

The use of outsiders

As you will have gathered, strategic workshops are a valuable tool but are deceptively complex. If the first one you hold is not as successful as you wish, learn from experience, and the next one will be significantly better.

A short-cut is to use an outsider with experience of successful workshops. He or she could be an external adviser, someone from another subsidiary or head office staff, or a non-executive director.

Sometimes a chief executive will use an outsider to a chair a strategic workshop. This can be appropriate when he feels there is a danger that he will direct the discussion more than he would wish.

An external adviser can be particularly helpful where either a company is performing unsatisfactorily or there is a lack of direction for the future. In such a case it is desirable that the external adviser carries out a confidential interview before the workshop with each person attending, to establish what are the obstacles to be overcome and to encourage people to suggest strategic options for future success.

Where the outsider is not chairing the workshop, then his role should be to:

● encourage people to say exactly what they think

● ensure that contentious aspects are faced up to and discussed openly where appropriate

● achieve rigour and clarity of thought in the discussions

● act as a catalyst to ensure that innovative ideas are put forward and considered constructively

● ensure that the action to be taken after the workshop is clearly specified and personal accountabilities assigned

● support the chairman of the workshop constructively and unobtrusively during the working sessions, and in the intervals in between, to achieve a successful outcome

129

Different uses of strategic workshops

It would be completely wrong to give the impression that because strategic workshops are complex events they are suitable only for companies with a sophisticated approach to strategic management. It has been proved that strategic workshops are the best way to introduce strategic approaches to managing a business by the success family businesses and professional partnerships have achieved with them. A strategic workshop should ensure that people adopt an integrated and co-ordinated approach to developing the business.

Frequency of strategic workshops

For a business about to adopt a strategic approach for the first time there is a strong case for holding two or three workshops at about 6-week intervals. The time between workshops should be used to progress matters in preparation for the next one.

In those businesses where there is a requirement to prepare a strategic plan annually, there is a temptation to hold only one workshop a year to begin the business-planning process. But those companies which have decided to hold an interim workshop at the mid-year stage have usually found it to be productive. It ensures that people continue to act as well as to think strategically.

Action summary

1. Use strategic workshops. They have proved to be successful for family businesses, professional partnerships, non-profit-making organisations, subsidiary companies and multi-nationals alike.

2. Keep the agenda to issues of strategic importance.

3. Put the most important item first on the agenda, not last.

4. Restrict the numbers attending to members of the executive committee.

5. Hold the workshop away from the office to avoid interruptions.

6. Ensure that actions of strategic importance result from the workshop, with personal accountability assigned.

7. Consider using an outsider to short-cut the inevitable learning process when using a workshop for the first time.

11 HOW TO MAKE THE VISION BECOME REALITY

The most effective way to achieve the vision is to stick to a simple and common-sense management style. The following ingredients make up the recipe for success:

- major business-development projects
- an effective organisational structure
- sound decisions for R&D expenditure and capital investment
- highly motivated, competent and committed staff throughout the organisation

These ingredients will be considered in turn.

Business-development projects

Evolutionary growth is unlikely to produce more than incremental improvement in results for many businesses today, because the growth within their market is correspondingly modest. Simply concentrating on today's problems and letting the future take care of itself is not therefore a recipe for success. Capital investment, revenue investment and management time are needed to achieve a quantum jump in the results achieved, in addition to a vision for success. Resources need to be harnessed by defining a handful of major business-development projects, with each one assigned to an individual member of the executive committee.

Measurable milestones of progress must be set for the next 12 months. In the rapidly changing business world of today it is inappropriate to set milestones to be achieved beyond that time. Further milestones should be set each year to achieve the eventual completion of long-term projects.

It must be recognised that business-developments projects often require the participation of more than one function or department of the business. This must not be allowed to become an excuse for delay. For example, the research director may need the help of the manufacturing department to produce prototypes of a product for field testing, and if he is accountable for the project, then it is his job to secure the necessary help from the manufacturing department. He is personally *accountable* for securing it, and any excuse is unacceptable.

Unless there is total commitment to business-development projects, the vision is likely to remain an idle dream. The definition of projects is so important that an example is given below.

An electronics company whose vision was to obtain a stock-market quotation within 3 years set the following milestones to be achieved within the next 12 months:

	Person responsible	Date
• Appoint major distributors to cover the USA and Germany	**Marketing director**	December
• Complete the prototype for a low-cost version of the major product	**Research director**	June
• Take over the manufacture of a major sub-assembly from an outside company and achieve a 20 per cent cost reduction as a result	**Manufacturing director**	September

	Person responsible	Date
● Relocate the business into larger premises	**Managing director**	July
● Complete the computerisation of inventory control	**Finance director**	October
● Change the auditors to a firm suitable for a company seeking a stock-market quotation	**Finance director**	September

For a company which is making a loss or performing unsatisfactorily the projects will need to be designed to achieve short-term improvements in profits and cash flow. For a successful company most of the projects are likely to be aimed at the medium term, and some of them will incur revenue expenses in the coming year rather than make a profit. It is important therefore that business-development projects are defined before budgeting begins, so that their impact is included.

Within each function of the business there should be a handful of development projects designed to achieve the vision for that part of the business. Some of these projects will be to achieve a separate part of one of the corporate business-development projects described above. Each project should be made the accountability of a senior manager within the function.

An effective organisational structure

A sound organisational structure is so important for success that it is a strategic issue. Common sense is much more use than academic theory for devising an effective organisation.

The organisational structure should follow certain basic principles:

● the minimum number of tasks should be done at head office, so that the number of corporate staff is kept to a minimum

135

- the company should be organised into separate strategic businesses, with different profit centres within each one, as appropriate

- profit-centre accountability requires control of sales, operations and research and development

- profit centres should be based on market segments rather than products to avoid businesses competing with each other

- too many individual profit centres and cost centres should be avoided

- a minimum number of organisational layers are needed, to make communication easier

- 'deputy' and 'assistant' appointments should be avoided, since they tend to blur personal accountability

- supporting and specialist services should be bought externally, where appropriate

These principles will be illustrated in turn, and then the creation of an effective organisational structure will be considered.

Head office

A blank sheet of paper is the best management tool for reviewing the organisational structure of head office. The starting point should be to assume that no head office is necessary. The role of head office should be established by answering the following questions:

- What tasks *must* be carried out at head office to meet statutory requirements?

- Which other roles should undeniably be carried out at head office?

- Why should any other function be done at head office?

- Where should those functions which may be described at 'head office' be located for maximum cost-effectiveness?

The starting point should be to assume that no head office is necessary

It is not only multi-nationals that fall into the trap of centralising too many people at head office. One company employing only a few hundred people is organised quite sensibly into three divisions based in different parts of the country, each one serving a different market segment, but it employs three management accountants at head office, each one assigned to 'look after' and help a particular division. This is nonsense. The management accountants should be located within the divisions and report to the divisional general manager, not to the group finance director. There is a niggling concern in the minds of the divisional general managers that the management accountants act as head-office spies on occasions, so they fail to consult the accountants as much as they should.

The aim should be to employ the minimum number of people centrally, and those people should be of the highest calibre. Wherever

137

possible, people should only spend a 2- or 3-year period at head office, before returning to a line-management job.

Strategic business

The essence of a strategic business is that it should be large enough:

- to have the resources under its own control to achieve success in a market sector and/or geographical region, which may be worldwide

- to have, or to plan to achieve, a significant market share or market leadership, as appropriate, within the geographical region to be served

- to be organised into separate profit centres, as appropriate, with each one serving a particular market segment, country or region

The strategic businesses should be sufficiently few in number and distinctive from each other to be easily perceived and understood by customers and investors alike. This is not to recommend a return to conglomerate groups. Only a small proportion of large conglomerates have demonstrated a record of sustained success over longer than a decade.

Strategic businesses for an electronics company, for example, may be quite distinctive from each other and yet related by nature. They could be:

- telecommunication systems

- radar

- military communication systems

- microelectronics

- consumer electronic products

- electronic systems for building management

Every effort must be made to avoid creating a second layer of la head-office staffs in each strategic business. The starting point should be to assume that a chief executive and financial director are the only *essential* members of the strategic business's head office. Any other person should be appointed only on the grounds of indisputable necessity to achieve the vision.

The number of profit and cost centres

Whilst personal accountability for a profit or cost centre is to be encouraged, one can have too much of a good thing. For example, one group with a turnover of about £50 million and 1,000 employees was organised into over 30 profit centres and some 200 cost centres. Because of the large number of different entities, there was a huge amount of transferred charges on an allocated cost basis. Managers complained that most of their costs were merely a transfer to them from a different cost centre, so they were not really accountable for costs. Worse still, few of the profit centres received adequate attention from the board. Needless to say, a large staff of accountants and data-processing people was employed to cope with the monthly management reporting.

Reorganisation of this group created five strategic businesses, with a total of nine divisions. The number of cost centres was reduced dramatically, the accountants and data-processing staff were redeployed, frustration caused by the old structure was reduced and morale improved all round.

Profit-centre accountability

The creation of individual profit centres offers the following advantages:

- personal accountability is increased
- more management-development opportunities are created

139

- a greater sense of local identification with the business by all staff is encouraged

Care must be taken in the creation of profit centres, otherwise the potential advantages may be lost. The prerequisite is that a profit centre must be accountable for sales. For example, if two so-called 'profit centres' share a common sales force, then accountability for profit does not exist separately; opportunities abound for the 'profit-centre managers' to blame the sales manager for non-performance, and vice versa. In an actual case one profit-centre manager criticised the sales manager for giving his products insufficient attention compared to the other profit centre, and the other one criticised the sales manager for a failure to win new accounts. The sales manager criticised both of them for inadequate product supply and slow delivery to customers. The problem was only overcome when one profit centre was created, by putting a chief executive in charge of the whole business.

In the same way, if the control of research and development does not rest with the profit centres, then accountability is reduced. If cost-effectiveness requires a central research and development facility, then responsibility for selecting projects and payment for them should be given to the profit centres as much as possible, except for centrally funded research projects.

The creation of profit centres must be based on serving the customer effectively. For example, a major company purchasing for nationwide outlets would expect to buy centrally, even if the supplier had regional profit centres.

Equally, where competing brands are organised into separate profit centres serving some common customers, care must be taken to ensure that:

- customers are happy to purchase separately

- the cost of selling, distribution and merchandising is not excessive

- competition between competing brands is beneficial

One effective way to create profit centres is in terms of separate market segments, each one serving a different group of customers rather than a product group. The market-segment approach can be particularly relevant for professional partnerships. For example, separate profit centres may be set up for the different needs of clients in terms of advertising agencies, the entertainment industry, trade unions, the franchising industry and so on. There is a benefit to the client as well, because he is being advised by someone with a considerable background experience of his particular industry.

Organisational layers

Organisational simplicity and directness of communication are important features. To achieve this the number of layers from top to bottom of a group and each strategic business within it should be kept to a minimum.

In an insurance company one 'section' of thirty-five actuaries was structured into five different organisational levels. This was merely an example of the in-built bureaucracy which existed throughout the organisation.

The existence of separate regional and divisional head offices should be avoided altogether. Otherwise head-office staff end up attempting to find out what is going on via 'intermediate head offices', and direct contact with businesses is lost.

Full-time appointment of deputies and assistants

Deputies and assistants should be avoided. Their existence is often indicative of overmanning and a lack of clear-cut personal accountabilities. It is much better for each person to have individual accountability and a job title reflecting his area of responsibility.

Supporting and specialist services

Some of the most successful companies concentrate almost exclusively on running their mainstream business. Examples are to be found amongst large multi-nationals as well as much smaller companies and professional partnerships, which subcontract peripheral services to outside specialists.

Supporting services should be evaluated against other options at least every 3 years. If nothing else, such an evaluation provides an external yardstick of cost-effectiveness. Any significant outlay on supporting services should be examined in this way, including:

- canteen and vending facilities
- cleaning services
- vehicle-fleet management
- distribution and delivery
- building maintenance
- security services
- chauffeur services
- energy management
- pension administration
- merchandising support

The external purchase of professional services should also be evaluated. It may well be possible to obtain a higher quality of service for the same cost in some instances. Specialist services departments that should be evaluated include:

- patents and trade marks
- legal advice
- public relations
- corporation tax

- artwork and graphic design
- architectural services

Creating an effective organisational structure

An effective organisational structure cannot be created by adherence to sound principles alone. The structure must be designed expressly to help turn the vision into reality. The energies of the whole staff must be harnessed to make the vision happen, and not dissipated by internal politics, which often result from an unsatisfactory organisational structure.

The steps required to develop an effective structure are:

- Define the vision and *the goals* to be achieved. For example, if a goal is that, say, overseas activities will contribute 25 per cent of group profits within 3 years, compared to under 5 per cent presently, then weight must be given to this in the organisation structure *now* to help make it happen.

- Select the strategic options to be pursued. For example, if it is decided to switch the emphasis from direct sales to customers to selling via distributors, then organisational change will be necessary.

- Identify internal obstacles to success, e.g. if the present policy of subcontracting of software design is causing unsatisfactory customer service.

- Review the present organisation to identify features to retain and aspects which need to be changed, e.g. if some divisions share a common sales force, which results in a lack of accountability.

The last step should be to review the present organisational structure, because this can only be done effectively in relation to visions, goals and obstacles which have been identified.

Once the organisational structure has been created, other features should be incorporated.

Interest should be charged to strategic businesses, on a notional basis if banking is centralised, to encourage people to pursue cash management to minimise the amount of money invested in the business.

Corporate overhead costs which are to be allocated should be charged as a 'budgeted, lump sum', to prevent the waste of senior management time debating about the method or fairness of the charges to be made. The actual costs each month are likely to be different from the budgeted amount, but the allocation should simply be on the budgeted lump sum basis, and the variance treated as the accountability to the department incurring the cost.

'Scarce' central resources provided for operating companies should be charged on a used basis to encourage sensible and economic use.

For example, a computer software design team providing a centralised internal service within a group could be charged out to users according to the time spent on each job done. This helps to promote efficiency and a value-for-money attitude by the people providing the service. A price for the job could be given to the user in advance and any subsequent cost over-run would have to be absorbed by the central department. Alternatively, if user departments receive a fixed charge, regardless of the extent they use the service, some are likely to think that the charges are unfair and others may be encouraged to use the service indiscriminately.

Research and capital-investment decisions

Common sense is needed just as much as technical expertise to make sound research and development decisions. Research and developments projects require market evaluation before expenditure is authorised. Otherwise there is a risk of inventing or developing something and then looking for a market. Questions to be answered before investing in development for a new product include:

- What is the size of the present market?

- How is the demand being satisfied now?

- If the demand is a latent one which has to be created, what are the available data to assess the potential market?

- What are the performance and price of existing products?

- What performance do customers want and how much are they prepared to pay?

- What other product developments are taking place by existing and possible future competitors?

- What rate of build-up of market share is anticipated?

- Will the product sell primarily to our existing customers?

- Will a separate distribution network or sales force be required?

- What is the expected cash-flow payback period or discounted cash-flow rate of return calculated on the total project expenditure of research, capital investment and working capital?

Although the evaluation will necessarily be based to some extent on guesswork, a comprehensive market and financial evaluation should be made at the outset. Any uncertainties increase the need for evaluation, not reduce it. 'What if' questions should be answered to test the sensitivity of the project. For example, what would the effect be on the return from the project *if*:

- The product launch takes 6 months longer to achieve than planned?

- Research and development costs are 10 per cent higher than expected?

- The working capital required is 20 per cent greater than expected because higher stock levels become necessary and customers take longer to pay than expected?

- Manufacturing costs are 2 per cent higher than forecast during the first year?

- The cost of warranty work is 5 per cent more than forecast after the first year?

- Sales are 10 per cent lower than forecast during the first 2 years?

- Selling prices have to be reduced by 3 per cent after the first year to combat competition?

During an important and lengthy R&D project the initial evaluation should be reassessed in the light of information gained as the project progresses.

Capital-expenditure investment of a significant amount should be subjected to written evaluation. The payback period or discounted cash-flow rate of return should be calculated on the total cash flow, including:

- capital expenditure

- working capital

- operating revenues and costs

- the impact elsewhere in the group, e.g. the distribution division will have to recruit extra staff and extend the North West regional depot to handle the additional sales volume

It is desirable to set different investment returns from different categories of projects to reflect their varying risk and uncertainty.

Suitable project categories may be:

- cost reduction or profit improvement from existing operations

- expansion of existing products in existing market segments and geographical territories

- a new product launch in an existing market segment or geographical territory

- a new product in a new segment or geographical territory

Clearly the *inherent* risk and uncertainty increases along with the degree of diversification. Whilst answering 'what if' questions is a worthwhile analysis, it does not reduce the risk of a speculative venture.

People submitting capital-expenditure proposals may become so entangled with the detail that they lose sight of the purpose of the investment. The proposal may be to buy a particular machine, when the purpose is to increase product availability. Obviously subcontracting and manufacturing under licence are some of other options available. It is essential therefore that those authorising capital investment should receive acceptable answers to the following questions:

- What is the fundamental purpose of the project?

- What other different approaches to achieve the purpose have been considered and rejected?

- What other alternative equipment and specifications to those recommended have been evaluated and rejected?

- Why should the investment be made now?

- What will be the advantages as well as the disadvantages of delaying the investment by 3 months, 6 months, or 12 months?

Many large companies devote a lot of management time to capital-project evaluation, and then do nothing to check whether performance is in line with the original proposal. This does not make sense. As the required returns from capital-expenditure projects are publicised within many companies, there is a temptation for managers to be over-optimistic on occasions in calculating the return required to obtain approval.

Major capital expenditure projects should be audited. The problem is that after a project is approved, the usual form of management reporting does not allow individual projects to be assessed. A separate project-progress report is needed.

Whenever a large project is approved by a board, then the timing of any ad hoc progress reports required should be specified. When it is known that actual achievement will be monitored from ae to time until success has been achieved, over-optimistic project proposals are less likely to be submitted.

Staff motivation and commitment

Staff prefer to work for a demonstrably successful business, one which is highly regarded for a professional approach. This demands that the highest standards of achievement and performance are displayed by top management to set a personal example and to demand similar standards from their staff. Yet some managers actually condone mediocrity by allowing unsatisfactory work to pass without comment.

Even small but important details must be actioned properly. For example, to accept a letter to a customer from your secretary with a typing error and to simply correct it by hand is *to condone mediocrity*.

At least three worthwhile benefits can come from paying people above average:

- high standards of performance
- existing staff are more likely to be retained
- it is easier to recruit staff of the required calibre

Management development and staff training should be regarded as an investment in the key asset of the business, namely people, and people who have attended courses need to have an early opportunity to put their learning into action. The purpose of management development and staff training should also be to help improve the financial performance of the business. So the money spent must be equally purposeful.

External management development and training courses need careful selection, otherwise they are one of the easiest ways to waste money. Tailor-made courses may be better value for money than standard external programmes because there can be greater concentration on what is needed.

The largest opportunity by far, however, for management development and staff training is planned work experience and accountability for specific projects, in addition to the normal job responsibilities. Some companies, such as Shell, have made a major commitment in this way and benefited accordingly. Many more companies should put more effort into these opportunities, and attach less reliance upon standard external training courses.

Share-option, share-purchase and profit-participation schemes should be pursued. It must be desirable for as many staff as possible to have a sense of ownership in the business, and to receive a

Every manager should seek to generate and inject excitement into his department

tangible and tax-efficient benefit as a result. Increasingly, unquoted companies are introducing similar schemes to help motivate and retain staff.

Excitement and enthusiasm are important ingredients to help motivate staff. Enthusiasm needs to be set by personal example from the top and then positively communicated to people. Enthusiasm is contagious. Excitement needs to be created. Every manager should seek to generate and inject excitement into his department.

Aids to generating excitement include:

- short-term sales campaigns with attractive prizes

- setting, publicising and then beating performance targets

- communicating successes such as important new orders or customers

- giving people demanding projects which provide a new challenge and widen their experience

- creating opportunities by opening new sales offices and launching new products

- encouraging people to come forward with ideas and giving them the opportunity to put worthwhile ones into practice themselves

- making acquisitions which create more career opportunities

All the above examples, however, must contribute to the achievement of the company vision as well as create excitement.

Action summary

1. Define major business-development projects and measurable progress milestones to complete during the next 12 months, with individual accountability for each one, to make the vision happen.

2. Minimise the number of staff employed centrally and concentrate on strategic-business and profit-centre accountability.

3. Evaluate research and development projects in market and financial terms before authorising expenditure.

4. Evaluate capital-expenditure projects in terms of the cash-flow payback period or the discounted cash-flow rate of return.

5. Carry out audits on major capital projects to ensure that satisfactory results are being achieved.

6. Generate excitement and enthusiasm as a conscious part of your management style.

12 HOW TO MAKE SUCCESSFUL MANAGEMENT BUY-OUTS AND BUY-INS

This chapter could *dramatically improve your personal wealth.*

Management *buy-outs* are commonplace in the USA and the UK, the largest examples running into billions of dollars. The American expression 'leveraged buy-out' is more accurate than the term management buy-out, because most of the finance is usually provided by institutions.

The members of the management team normally:

- invest some of their own money, often borrowed against the equity in their homes or with the collateral of insurance policies

- obtain a significant equity stake in the company, disproportionately much higher than their personal investment of cash

- can increase their equity stake by achieving performance targets, often referred to as a 'ratchet mechanism'

- have executive management control of the business, though the financial institutions usually appoint a non-executive director to represent their interests

In the UK management buy-outs have grown rapidly, the largest having cost well over £100 million each. More than 100 financial institutions provide finance for management buy-outs.

In contrast, management *buy-ins* are much less common in the UK, but are increasing. If you cannot achieve a management buy-out of your own company, you should consider seeking a buy-in opportunity.

A management buy-in requires a proven track record in a closely related market sector. Some successful buy-in teams have consisted of only two people, usually a chief executive and a finance director. The first step is to find a suitable target company which can be purchased.

You may still be unsure why a management buy-out or buy-in could affect your personal wealth. The reasons are:

- Financial institutions want to realise their investment within 5 years by your selling the company or obtaining a stock-market quotation. If an attractive opportunity to realise the investment arises much earlier, usually they will want to take it unless the management can convince them of the extra benefit from retaining the investment longer.

- The record of success has been very high, but of course there have been disappointments and failures.

- Managers have *multiplied their original investment tens of times* in the most successful cases.

Buy-outs and buy-ins really do offer the opportunity to create substantial personal capital within 5 years. They could therefore provide you with *a golden opportunity to realise your vision for personal wealth and success*.

The initiative for a management buy-in must come from the managers themselves, and many buy-outs also arise from the initiative of the management team. Groups are prepared to consider divestment, including management buy-outs, for various reasons, including:

- the business is an unwanted part of a larger acquisition

- it may no longer fit into the present commercial rationale for the group

- the business may be too small to carry the overhead costs associated with a separate profit centre of a large group

. . . Multiplied their original investment tens of times

- the market is simply too competitive to carry the full weight of corporate overhead

- the need to generate more cash or the wish to invest the proceeds in other opportunities

Other opportunities for management buy-outs, and possibly buy-ins as well, include:

- privatisation of state-owned corporations

- the purchase of a listed company, particularly where there are substantial family shareholdings and members of the family are approaching retirement

- an alternative to an unwelcome bid for a listed company
- purchase of a company in receivership

Despite the availability of opportunities, and the substantial potential rewards, common sense demands that a hard-headed and objective approach is adopted by the management team.

Suitable companies for a management buy-out or buy-in

The essential ingredients for a suitable company are:

- cash flow
- asset backing
- the business
- the management team

Each aspect will be considered in turn.

Cash flow

Cash flow is the most vital consideration. Unless it is demonstrated that sufficient cash can be generated to pay the substantial amount of interest and repay loan finance when necessary, a deal is not possible.

It must be realised that the reason why the management team obtains a much higher proportion of equity than its members' contribution to the total funding is because a substantial amount of loan finance and overdraft facility is used to make the purchase. So a business which is likely to need significant injections of cash during the next few years is unsuitable for a buy-out deal. This means that businesses in relatively mature industrial sectors are usually more suitable than those in young, high-growth and high-technology sectors, unless such a business can be managed in a way to generate cash: for example, by using distributors to stock the hardware and to install complex electronic systems which would require a substantial amount of working capital. However, in that case the distributors are making a sizeable share of the profit the company could be making for itself, and profit, unfortunately, is secondary to the need to generate sufficient cash flow to service the loan capital.

Asset backing

As a substantial amount of loan finance and overdraft facility will be used to finance the purchase, it is essential that there are sufficient tangible assets in the business to provide adequate security for the lenders. Service companies that are low on asset backing and heavily dependent on retaining key fee-earners may well be unsuitable. Not only is there the lack of security for the lender but there is an added risk that key people who are not part of the management team making the investment may leave. Increasingly, whole teams of people leave companies either as a result of head-hunting or to start their own business. In either of these circumstances a significant proportion of their clients may follow them.

The business

A suitable company must have a long-term future. The sale of the business or obtaining a stock-market quotation could take up to 5 years. Then the purchasers or new investors will want to see continuing prospects, so the cash flow generated has to be sufficient to pay interest charges, to provide for investment in replacement equipment and new technology to remain competitive, and to improve existing products and develop new ones where necessary.

The business may be making only a modest profit, producing a loss or be in receivership at present. This does not necessarily mean the company is unsuitable. A clearly thought-out plan will be needed, however, to show how sufficient profit can be achieved to help generate the necessary cash flow.

Factors which may make this feasible include:

- eliminating central service charges and providing the necessary facilities within the business at a much lower cost
- identifying specific and achievable cost-reduction opportunities
- defining opportunities to generate additional turnover from the existing facilities

Significant amounts of business with other group companies may be a cause of vulnerability. The management team should not expect favoured treatment as an independent company.

The management team

People talk glibly about management teams all the time. Management teamwork is essential for a buy-out or buy-in. Members of the team need to be a close-knit group totally committed to making their vision for success become a reality.

Investors look for credibility in the management team. If the business is presently producing unsatisfactory results, the investors will want to know why and how the same people will be able to achieve a turn-around. A competent financial director capable of ensuring cash-flow discipline is essential, but there should be no key appointment missing from the management team. If the technical director has just left, for instance, this may have caused a serious weakness that will not be easily overcome.

Making the approach

Management buy-outs and buy-ins will be considered separately, as different approaches are required.

Management teamwork is essential

Management buy-outs

Determination at the start is one of the most crucial aspects of a management buy-out. The commitment of the chosen management team and their willingness and ability to raise some personal finance must be established conclusively at that point. Otherwise an unnecessary risk is being taken. The group may be upset at the suggestion of a management buy-out, and there is no point in taking this risk unless there is a determination to proceed.

One way to avoid this risk is for an external adviser to enquire whether or not a group is prepared to sell a business, without disclosing the identity of the bidder unless the group is prepared to consider a deal. This kind of approach is made frequently on behalf of corporate acquirers and is becoming increasingly common for management buy-outs. It is reasonable to expect the external adviser to make the initial approach without charge unless agreement to proceed is obtained.

Management buy-ins

A management buy-in requires a different approach, for the target company may well be listed on a stock exchange. When an approach is made to a target company, whether it is quoted on a stock exchange or not, the prospective vendors will want an assurance that sufficient funds are available before exploring a possible sale of their business. It is important that the management buy-in team has made contact with prospective investors before contacting a target company. In this way they will be more convincing to a prospective vendor and able to complete the deal more quickly. Additionally, some buy-in investors know of companies which would be amenable to an approach, provided that a suitable management team is available.

Using an outside adviser

There is likely to be a strong tendency to reject outside advice and help in order to minimise expense, but the management team should recognise that it is facing a number of new challenges. They must be able:

- to negotiate the purchase with their present employers *on equal terms*, knowing that if a deal does not take place they will wish to remain as employees

- to obtain the necessary corporation tax and financial advice to decide upon the maximum price which should be paid for the business and how to structure the tax deal effectively

- to select a suitable institutional investor from the large number available

- to present themselves, and their business plan, convincingly to prospective investors

- to negotiate the best deal for themselves with the institutional investor

- to choose a firm of company commercial lawyers experienced in these deals

An outside adviser should play a leading part in tackling the above challenge successfully. The advantages he should provide include:

- making an anonymous initial approach to the parent company

- providing the valuation and corporation-tax expertise needed

- taking a tough negotiating stance when necessary with the parent company

- choosing the three of four most relevant buy-out investors, from the dozens which exist, for the management team to meet and to make their personal choice of financial partner

- having enough experience to know how attractive a deal can be negotiated with the investors on behalf of the management team

- recommending a partner in a law firm with relevant experience

The choice of institutional investor is important, for there is much more to it than negotiating a one-off financial transaction. The investor will wish to appoint a non-executive director, possibly the person in charge of the investment or someone from its pool of available non-executive directors. It is important that the person appointed is compatible with the management team. Ideally, he should make a positive contribution to the business and not merely be a watchdog.

The choice of institutional investor will be put to the test if things start to go seriously wrong. The investor will want to see prompt and vigorous corrective action taken. In choosing among investors, therefore, the management team should ask how they have responded in situations where a company has faced a serious setback. The approach of different institutional investors varies widely: some are prepared to be patient, passive and tolerant, whereas others may seek to intervene decisively.

Timescale

Once a buy-out or buy-in has been agreed in principle, speed is essential, or the business is likely to suffer. Uncertainty may lower morale amongst the staff. Less attention will be given to managing the business whilst the negotiations are taking place.

As an indication, 3 or 4 months should be sufficient to complete the transaction from initial agreement in principle. If the deal is in response to an unwelcome bid for a listed company, then a quicker completion is likely to be essential.

Business plan

The purpose of the business plan should be to provide the information and forecasts for:

- institutional investors to help them decide to invest
- the purchase price to be decided
- the financial structure of the deal to be determined

The plan should be written by the management team, and must provide a comprehensive picture. The outside advisers should provide guidance and review it to ensure it is an effective document to help sell the deal to investors.

Investors do not expect everything to go according to plan, so they expect to see:

- risk areas and uncertainties identified

- plans to avoid potential problems, or to minimise their impact

- contingency plans if problems do occur

- sensitivity analysis to answer 'what if' questions

The presentation of the document should be professional, attractive and readable, it should be bound effectively, and there should be an index. Published material such as product literature and press comment should be included in an appendix. The temptation to go into too much detail, resulting in too long a document, must be avoided. The first page of the plan should give a *one-page executive summary* of the entire proposal. All this may sound like common sense, but basic errors are often made. There may be no executive summary, the size of investment required may not even be mentioned, and duplicated copies of published material may be difficult to read.

The content of the plan should include:

- Executive summary, a single page which tells the prospective investor in outline everything he needs to know to decide whether he could be interested or not

- The company
  - history
  - present ownership
  - location
  - key products and services
  - suitability for a buy-out or buy-in
  - commercial rationale for making the proposed investment

- The market place, marketing and selling
  - the size of the market place and forecast growth
  - competition and a comparative assessment of products and services in terms of performance and pricing

    – major customers and distributors
    – marketing, selling and sales-promotion plans

Where appropriate, published sources of information should be quoted to support estimates and forecast growth of the market segment. Comparative product performance could be supported by reprints from test reports published in consumer magazines and the trade press. Such reprints should be included in an appendix.

- Manufacturing and distribution
  - land and buildings
  - production facilities
  - use of latest technology
  - surplus capacity
  - need for additional capital investment
  - key suppliers and subcontractors
  - warehousing and distribution

- Technical
  - current and proposed R&D projects
  - patents, licences and trademarks
  - anticipated technological developments within the industry and the planned response

- People
  - members of the buy-out team
  - organisational structure
  - other key employees and expertise
  - headcount analysis by department
  - employee relations and trade unions

- Financial summary
  - estimated purchase price and expenses
  - anticipated time to realise the investment and likely exit routes
  - working-capital requirements
  - historical and forecast profit and loss accounts and cash-flow figures, covering the next 3 years
  - budgeting, monthly-reporting and financial-management procedures

The appendices should include the following information:

- Financial. Detailed projections of profit and loss and cash flow for the next 3 years, supported by a statement of all assumptions used and sensitivity analysis.

- Management biographies. Factual biographies of each member of the buy-out or buy-in team and other key managers and staff. Qualifications, previous employers, positions held and tangible achievement should be detailed. Waffle should be avoided.

- Published information
  - product and service brochures
  - press comment and articles

Negotiating the deal

There is much more to be negotiated than simply agreeing a purchase price. The deferral of part of the purchase consideration, the structure of the deal, tax implications, conditions, warranties and indemnities may affect the total cost and attractiveness of the deal significantly.

The first matter for negotiation is an exclusive option period, where the company is not listed on a stock exchange. This means that an auction situation will be avoided. If there is a competitive bid, the purchase price required is likely to be higher. In addition, the added uncertainty may well damage morale within the company.

Key matters to be resolved in addition to the purchase price include:

- the use and cost of central services which will be needed for an interim period until alternative facilities are created within the company, e.g. data-processing

- rights to intellectual property such as patents, trademarks, trade names and licences

- the cost of any redundancies
- the transfer of pension-scheme benefits
- the structure of the deal and the tax implications for both parties
- warranties and indemnities

In most cases tough and expert negotiation is needed to achieve a satisfactory price for a buy-out or a buy-in. The burden of debt interest means there is usually a fine dividing line between an acceptable purchase price and one which prohibits a deal altogether.

When agreement has been reached, the investors and lenders will normally require an accountants' report to be prepared by a suitable firm. It is the accountants' report rather than the business plan on which the investors will formally commit themselves.

In the case of a buy-out the management team's knowledge of the business used to prepare the business plan should mean that there are no significant adverse disclosures in the accountants' report. In a management buy-in, however, the business plan has to be written much more on an arm's length basis; so there is a greater likelihood that the deal is renegotiated or the financial structure amended as a result of the accountants' report.

Staff

Motivation and morale should improve following a management buy-out or buy-in. There is a risk, however, that a 'them and us' attitude could develop, separating the management team that has invested in the business from the remainder of the management and staff.

Serious consideration should be given to creating staff-incentive schemes on the completion of the deal. Depending upon current tax regulations, attractive incentives schemes may be provided by:

- profit-sharing
- share options

● saving-based share purchases

It is nothing less than enlightened self-interest to err on the generous side when creating incentives for management and staff in either a management buy-out or buy-in deal. You will benefit from, and probably need, every bit of goodwill, co-operation and commitment to help make your vision of personal wealth come true.

Action summary

1.	Consider initiating a management buy-out of your company, provided that cash flow can be generated and asset backing exists to support the necessary borrowing.
2.	Consider a management buy-in of a suitable company in a similar industry, if your attempts at a buy-out are rejected.
3.	Recognise that cash-flow management is crucial in any buy-out or buy-in.
4.	Use external advice to help negotiate the best deal for yourself.
5.	Consider setting up profit-sharing and equity incentives for staff at the outset to ensure maximum co-operation and commitment.

INDEX

The Mercury titles on the pages that follow may also be of interest.
All Mercury books are available from booksellers or, in case of
difficulty, from:

Mercury Books
Gold Arrow Publications Ltd
862 Garratt Lane
London SW17 0NB

Further details and the complete catalogue of Mercury business
books are also available from the above address.

Also by Barrie Pearson . . .

COMMON-SENSE TIME MANAGEMENT

Time management is vital because success requires more than doing tasks
effectively and efficiently. Time must be found to persuade, motivate and
influence people as well.

Fortunately, every person is given the same amount of time each day. Time is
your most precious resource, and in this respect you are equal to the most
successful people who have ever lived. Forget the idea that education and
money determine success; they merely affect where you start from.

The crucial first step for you to take, however, is a conscious choice of the
success you want. Then you need to believe you *will* achieve it and you must
really *want* to achieve it. Action is essential to translate your vision and belief
into reality.

This book is first and foremost about your own personal success. It spells out
both the ingredients and action needed for you to achieve the success you want.

Using the techniques he has developed, Barrie Pearson has become an
outstandingly successful management consultant and seminar speaker. He is
Managing Director of Livingstone Fisher Plc, Management Consultants,
London.

ISBN 1–85251–046–3   **£14.95**

WHO CARES WINS

How to unlock the hidden potential in people at work . . . and turn ordinary companies into winners.

By Peter Savage, with foreword by Sir John Egan

Today's winner is without question the company that shows how to utilise the men and women at its disposal more effectively than its competitors can utilise theirs. In *Who Cares Wins*, a practical guidebook to modern management, Peter Savage draws on his own extensive experience to explain how anyone can master the art of group motivation. His step-by-step outline of the key to effective man-management looks at the problems and challenges confronting modern managers and supervisors at every level from the chief executive down, and considers how recent theories of 'excellence' can be transformed into practical and profitable reality.

Savage looks in detail at the right ways and wrong ways of approaching personal relationships at work. He explains how to create a platform for change, then looks at how it can be used, with spectacular results, to unlock unexpected extra energy from colleagues and employees. He identifies this crucial hidden energy as 'discretionary potential' – that piece of ourselves we all take to work but more often than not don't bother to apply. We all know already there are more effective ways of working within organisations large and small: *Who Cares Wins* is the story of how to achieve them.

ISBN 1–85252–015–9   £6.99

IF ONLY I HAD SAID . . .
Conversation control skills for managers

By Charles Margerison

How can you become more effective in your relationships with others? You can start by knowing how to control conversations.

What you say and how you say it is a key to success. This is particularly so when you are in a managerial position responsible for getting a team of people to work together. Business conversations can be won or lost depending on how you communicate. The techniques for success depend on recognising cues and clues, signs and signals, assumptions and assertions along with other key messages.

This book teaches you how to respond effectively using time dynamics, problem and solution-centred behaviour, requests and statements, and other methods such as parallel and sequential conversation.

This is the manager's handbook of how to become more effective in your dealings with people. It enables you to get your message across and understand others more quickly. You will be able as a result to get more done in less time – and what you do will be accepted and more effectively implemented than before.

The book is based on years of practical work with managers. The case examples illustrate practical uses in sales, production, personnel, research, marketing and training. Special exercises are provided for you to assess your own conversation control skills.

ISBN 1–85252–012–4

£5.99

CALL YOURSELF A MANAGER!

By Matthew Archer

Throughout the business world there are thousands of people trying desperately hard to become 'a manager'. Some of those who have made it to a management position have aspirations of becoming the 'chief executive'. It is not too difficult to acquire the technical knowledge that goes with the job but the human element is much more elusive: managers, being human, are subject to their own weaknesses and their performance can be affected by their fears, prejudices, lifestyle and relationships with others.

In this book, based on long experience (the examples are real – if disguised) the author analyses a wide range of management styles. In an amusing and readable manner, the author gives busy managers useful and practical advice on how to improve their performance and how to make both their own working lives and those of their staff more enjoyable and productive.

ISBN 1–85252–000–0   **£4.95** (paperback)

STRESS MANAGEMENT TECHNIQUES

Managing people for Healthy Profits.

By Dr Vernon Coleman

In an average lifetime the average employee loses one and a half years from work because of stress-induced illness. The result is that stress costs British industry £20,000,000,000 a year – far more than is lost through strikes or industrial disputes.

'Britain,' says Dr Vernon Coleman, 'leads the world in expensive, stress-induced disease.' He points out that if a company employs just 100 people then stress will cost that company around £400 a day. In a company which employs 1,000 people stress costs £1,000,000 a year.

Whatever else you try, and however much you spend on equipment, nothing will improve your company's efficiency and profitability more than taking care of your employees and reducing their unnecessary exposure to stress.

In *Stress Management Techniques* Dr Vernon Coleman explains exactly how, why and when stress causes problems. More importantly, he also explains exactly how you can control and minimise the amount of stress in your company.

Stress Management Techniques is illustrated with case histories and packed with easy-to-follow practical advice.

There have been many books about stress before. This book is unique in that it explains exactly how you can keep stress in your company to a minimum.

ISBN 1–85251–036–6   £9.95